INTRODUCTION

The human mind is undeniably complex—it is responsible for everything that we are as people. It determines who we are, what we like, and how we interact with the world. It determines how we behave and why we do what we do. It is complex enough for us all to have very distinctive personalities. However, despite this complexity, the human mind is surprisingly predictable. We may have our own differences, but at the heart of it all, our minds work with the same tendencies. Humans are surprisingly malleable. They can be convinced to do just about anything with ease. You can influence someone else, without them realizing what you are doing, in all sorts of different ways. From changing what you have said to changing your body language to altering the way that you talk, you can alter the way people respond.

This is hardly anything new—if you are a salesperson, you have probably been guided through ways that you can frame how you respond to those around you to try to get them to buy. If you work with children, you have probably been taught what you need to do in order to help facilitate a learning environment that will help them. If you work in law enforcement or something else that will involve you needing to exert your authority, you are taught the ways that you can use your body language to be seen as dominant as well. Ultimately, you can make use of how you act, how you speak, and the way that you hold yourself to ensure that you are able to control the way that other people respond. This is primarily because, while people can think and act on their own, the vast majority of what we do and how we feel is directly related to the way in which we respond unconsciously.

By being able to take advantage of the unconscious mind, you are able to control other people. You can take control of other people. You are able to come up with the ways that you can influence the way other people think, and in taking control of their thoughts, you are able to take control of their actions as well. This book is going to guide you through this process. You will be introduced to how manipulation, as a form of social influence, works. You will learn about what manipulation is as well as the ethicality about manipulation. While manipulation is not necessarily good or bad itself, it can be used in ways that are positive or negative for other people. You will learn how to manipulate other people effectively, and you will be guided through the role that emotions play in being able to manipulate others. You will then be guided through several very different forms of emotional manipulation and how they work. You will be guided through several different methods that can be used to manipulate others.

In particular, you will take a look at emotional manipulation to allow you to better influence behaviors. You will learn about methods of mind control and how you can genuinely control the ways that people interact with others. You will take a look at

Neuro-Linguistic Programming, a method that is used to influence how people around you interact by tapping into their unconscious minds. You will learn to understand the power of persuasion and how you can better influence the way that you will be able to control others without them ever realizing it. Finally, you will learn how you can use your body language and the way in which you hold yourself to help you influence everyone else.

Being able to influence and control other people can be incredibly useful. It can help you to learn how to better influence others to guide them to making decisions that are right for them. In being able to influence other people, you are able to ensure that, at the end of the day, you are in control. You can influence someone to do what you know is best for them. If you know that someone is more likely to act in a way that would be harmful or not benefit someone else in some way, you will be able to change the ways in which they are more likely to behave. Doctors can use this to encourage people to make treatment options that are right for them. Sales-people can encourage people to purchase other items. If you have a friend that is especially prone to making bad decisions, you can influence them as well—and this book will teach you to do exactly that.

Remember, the actions of others is dependent upon the ways in which you encourage other people to behave. The way that you approach other people can directly influence how others behave. It can allow you to change the way that people behave, but you also need to remember that, at the end of the day, you ought to respect the ways in which people think. You should respect the fact that people should, by and large, have that autonomy that they deserve. If you do choose to manipulate other people, you must accept that you are taking that risk for yourself. You must recognize that the consequences that come with it will be yours to take. Nevertheless, it could be that sometimes, the risk is worth it. Sometimes, it could be worth it to spend time manipulating others, and if you think that is the case, then that is your own prerogative.

WHAT IS MANIPULATION?

HAVE you ever had a time in which you wished more than anything that you would be able to control what other people were doing? Perhaps you desperately wanted to figure out how to get someone to do something for you. Or maybe, you wanted to help someone else to get them to do what you believed would be right for them. No matter the reason why, you may have desperately wanted to be able to control someone else.

That is not actually outside of the realm of possibility— you can learn how to influence and control other people, and it is not as hard as you may have initially thought. Manipulation can allow you to literally mold other behaviors. Manipulation allows for you to change the way that people are going to behave in several other ways. It will allow you to convince people to act in certain ways. It can allow you to even change the way in which other people think, allowing you to literally change the thoughts in the minds of others.

. . .

7

*W*ithin this chapter, you will take a closer look at what manipulation is. You will learn all about how it exists as a form of social influence and you will also look at some of the most common reasons that people choose to manipulate those around them. When you read through this chapter, you will want to keep in mind that this is the background information that you will need. You will see the ways in which manipulation exists and how it works. You will also understand the reasons that are commonly used to manipulate other people as well.

Social Influence and Manipulation

Ultimately, manipulation exists as a method of social influence. Social influence itself is the way in which people will naturally change their actions and behaviors depending upon the social environment that they are in. When you give in to social influence, you are most likely to be changing the way that you are acting in response to something else that happened around you. That could be in response to what someone else has asked or said to you. It could be in response to the actions of someone else. It could also be in response to what you believe that those around you think or will do.

*G*enerally speaking, there are three primary methods of social influence. These are compliance, identification, and internalization. Each works slightly differently, but they both work to make use of two inherent needs that people have—the need to be right and the need to be liked, both of which we will be discussing in more depth later.

. . .

Compliance

This refers to the appearance of agreeing but not actually agreeing in theory. You may act in the way that was requested of you, but you are not going to actually believe in it. For example, imagine that you are currently being asked to change a policy at work—perhaps you are told that you must refuse to serve anyone wearing purple and green shirts. If they are wearing both purple and green, you are told that you must not allow them to enter your store. Despite the fact that you may think that the rule is silly or is something that should not be enforced, you do force the point simply because you believe that you must follow through with what you were told to do. After all, if you do not comply with the whims of your employer, you will simply no longer have one. The result is that you will tell other people that they cannot shop in your store on the basis of the color of their clothing. You tell them that if they change their clothing, they can come in, but if not, they cannot enter. You apologize for the rule and say that you disagree with it, but you have no choice but to follow along. After all, you still have bills to pay. You still have mouths to feed. You need to work. This is compliance—you act as if you are in agreement even if your true thoughts on the matter are contradictory.

Internalization

Internalization, on the other hand, is meant to influence the way in which people think and act at the same time.

It is the attempt to change the thoughts of someone else while also encouraging the change of behaviors as well. It is essentially getting people to agree with you and the thoughts that you have. It is asking people to change the way in which you are able to think and act at the same time. Think about it this way—you are being asked to change your belief in something that you are doing. Perhaps you were told that you cannot eat meat on the job at your place of employment, and then in tandem with telling you that you cannot eat meat on the job, your manager also educated you on the reasons that you should not consume meat at all. If you were to agree that the reasons for not eating meat were valid, you have internalized the message—you believe that it is right to avoid eating meat, and so you change your habits as well.

Identification

Identification is a little bit different from the other two. With this particular form of social influence, you are relying on the fact that people will naturally be influenced by people that they admire. When someone admires someone else, such as a celebrity, they naturally want to align with the thoughts and beliefs of the one that they identify with. The result is that ultimately, when they do relate to someone else, they are going to attempt to emulate them. After all, mimicry is one of the most sincere forms of flattery, and when you mimic a celebrity or someone else that you admire, you are being influenced.

Manipulation

When it comes down to it, then, manipulation is the act of changing someone else's thoughts, feelings, or behaviors without them being aware of it. It is being able to change how someone is acting, essentially pulling their strings and influencing them directly. It is attempting to influence the other person to change either their thoughts or behaviors through methods that are oftentimes considered indirect or deceptive. Because manipulation works primarily by keeping the other person out of the loop, it is able to become quite effective very quickly—it is essentially escaping detection to allow for manipulation to occur.

The defining factor of manipulation, then, is that it relies on the person being manipulated to not know that they are being manipulated. This is oftentimes done through covert aggression, but not always. It can sometimes be done to advance the betterment of the manipulator, but not always. It can sometimes work in ways that harm the individual being manipulated, but not always.

Reasons to Manipulate

Ultimately, people use manipulation because they want to see a change in either the behaviors of someone else or they want to see a change in the thoughts of someone else. They are usually driven by one of several reasons, but the end result is oftentimes exactly the same—they want to change someone else. They want someone to behave differently for some reason, or they want someone to think differently for some reason or another. As you will read through this section, you will notice that some of these are more insidious than others. Some of the most common reasons to manipulate others include:

- **For advancing one's own purposes:** Some people find that they are entirely comfortable with taking advantage of other people. They treat those around them like steps to get further and further in life without struggling. These people generally do not empathize with others—they simply view other people as people to be abused and controlled, or as tools to allow them to get further ahead.

- **For power:** Some people feel like they need to get ahead and they need to feel powerful to do so. They feel like they are only secure in themselves when they have that feeling of superiority. They will intentionally manipulate people, not because they need something else, but because they want to feel that power over the other person for their own benefit. This is very dangerous—these kinds of people do not care about others. They have no qualms with hurting other people and they will not hesitate to do it. They think that the peace of mind that they get from doing so will be worth it.

- **For control:** Similarly to needing power, other people do so to control those around them. They feel like they are only able to remain stable and in control if they are able to exert that level of control onto those around them. It becomes very common, then, to see people that will reach out to control other people so they are able to feel better in general. Control gives people a sense that they are not entirely helpless. It allows people to ease their own anxiety about something when they feel like they can take control of something around them—even if that something is someone else.

- **For fun:** Some people simply want to control those around them because they feel like it will be fun. They are often bored or they want to do something to change up the monotony of life, so they turn manipulation into a game. They decide that they will simply move forward by attempting to figure out how to interact with others. They will, for example, try to get someone to do something else just to see if they can do it—it becomes like a challenge for them.

- **Unintentionally:** Some people inadvertently end up manipulating others. They do not mean to—it happens because they are unable to identify with the emotions of those around them. They oftentimes do not actually attempt to manipulate other people, but it winds up happening anyway due to problems with self-control, self-awareness, and lacking that essential element of empathy.

- **Impulsively:** Some people choose to manipulate entirely impulsively. They do it on a whim without actually planning it out. They are not attempting to be destructive —they just lack the self-control over their behaviors. They may, in response, however, also manipulate people in an attempt to preserve their image that would otherwise be challenged by the impulsive behaviors in the first place.

- **For some covert agenda:** Sometimes, the manipulation is very intentional and happens in order to manipulate someone into doing something that will fit an agenda. For example, think of those scammer phone calls that go out when people decide to manipulate others that are more likely to be vulnerable into doing something for them or to get them to pay for gift cards and mail them somewhere.

THE ETHICS OF MANIPULATION

CONSIDER THIS—YOU are talking to your best friend. Your friend is talking about how much she hates her boyfriend. She hates him and hates everything about him, and yet she refuses to break up with him. Is it wrong to heavily influence her to break up with him? Some people would have very different answers to this.

Ultimately, the ethicality of manipulation is a bit of a difficult concept to discuss and can be deemed widely open and dependent upon the context. When you are thinking about manipulating someone else, you may care whether what you are doing is morally objectionable or if it is something that would be permissible. The answer to this depends widely on intent. However, let's briefly note that manipulation itself is nothing more than a tool.

Like a gun or another weapon, manipulation itself is neutral—it is neither good nor bad. It is neither something to be avoided, nor is it something to be applauded or encouraged. At the end of the day, determining the morality of manipulation requires a debate on the reasoning behind it. Of course, you will have some people firmly stating that it is always bad—you see this with just about everything. In fact, there are people who would argue that alcohol, tobacco, and even caffeine, are always bad and therefore should always be avoided. There are people who will think that things are bad in just about any context. However, the truth of the matter is that there are many more nuances to what happens around you. It is not as simple as whether or not everyone agrees with something —it is whether or not *you* agree with it.

Think about it this way—if you know that someone is planning to go on a mass shooting attack, but you have the power to manipulate them into not doing so, is it wrong to manipulate them? Is it wrong to use that ability for a noble cause to prevent them from harming other people? Is it wrong to manipulate someone because you want to and you are bored?

What you have to consider here is the greater good of what you are doing. You cannot take an extreme perspective on this because, like all other great and difficult subjects, the judgment on manipulation is largely based on a spectrum. It is neither good nor bad on its own and you will need to consider the intentions behind the actions for hwy you are manipulating someone else, and that will require you to consider whether or not you trust what other people are doing, whether or not you are hurting other people with the way you are behaving, and so much more.

Some people will use manipulation in a way that is wrong or evil— they will use their manipulative tactics to grant them power or to get people to behave in ways that are wrong and there is no way around it. These are people who may try to manipulate you into giving them your money in an attempt to scam you. These people do not care about you and are entirely uninterested in understanding or reconciling with the morality behind those behaviors. The fact that you were impacted by them becomes entirely irrelevant and they do not bother with trying to fix the problem or change their behaviors. What matters to them is that they get what they want.

However, sometimes, manipulation can be justifiable. If you are ultimately serving the greater good, you have to consider whether or not what you are doing is worthwhile. You have to consider if what you are doing is going to benefit more people. It may be that your manipulation is going to save lives, such as if you were to stop someone from doing something dangerous. You could have, for example, prevented someone from behaving in a way that is harmful to many people by manipulating them just enough that you will be able to control the outcome of what is about to happen. If your manipulation occurs because you are attempting to stop someone from doing something harmful, or even something that is not in their own best interest, you have to recognize the value in doing what you have done.

Ultimately, manipulation is morally questionable at best—you could make the argument that it is *never* acceptable to manipulate others, no matter how many lives will be saved and no matter how much you can change an outcome for the better. However, it is also possible to argue against that point as well. If you are interested in the debate on whether or not you can justify the manipulation that you do to other people, then you will need to consider if you have the mental fortitude to follow through with it.

Manipulation is, inherently, something that is deceptive. It is inherently underhanded. If you believe that deception and under-handed behaviors are unacceptable, then you may not want to move forward with manipulation. If you are not interested in being able to interact with other people in ways that they are unaware of, you may not want to keep going forward. We will be addressing, in the next chapter, that in order to manipulate people, you must also be able to maintain a degree of ruthlessness that not everyone is comfortable with. If you cannot do that, then you may want to look at another method for influencing other people—and that is okay. Other forms of influence do exist, such as being able to influence through the use of persuasion or through the use of body language that do not carry with them that same degree of underhandedness that you may see in these methods.

At the end of the day, it will be up to you to decide on the ethics for yourself. However, one thing is for sure—if you are manipulating people for your own gain and inflicting harm on someone else, there is a good chance that what you are doing should probably be avoided if at all possible. If what you are doing is something that could get you into legal trouble, it probably is something that is not ethically permissible.

Keep in mind, however, that manipulation itself will remove autonomy from someone else—this sets it apart from persuasion, which allows for that autonomy to be maintained. When you manipulate someone else, you are simply giving them the illusion of a choice—sure, they can choose how they will behave, but you are also approaching them in a way that will directly change the way that they behave. You are working with the understanding of how the brain works to figure out how you can best push them to do what it is that you want the most. That revocation of autonomy is a major violation of their inherent rights as a person that must be considered while you weigh the pros against the cons.

HOW TO MANIPULATE EFFECTIVELY

Now, with the ethicality and the understanding of what manipulation is out of the way, it is time to start delving into the important details. Within this chapter, we are going to take a look at what goes into manipulation in order to make sure that it is successful at the end of the day. This chapter is going to emphasize and focus on the ways in which you will be able to alter the behaviors and thoughts of other people. You will be guided through the three criteria that are necessary in order to determine whether or not manipulation is successful. These can be thought of as determining factors that will really aid in being able to manipulate effectively in the first place. After that, we will take a look at some of the most common methods of manipulation that exist.

Criteria for Successful Manipulation

When it comes down to manipulating people, you may be wondering what it is that you can do to ensure that you are better able to control other people. There are a few different ways that you can ensure that your manipulation is successful, and ultimately there are three primary criteria that you must meet in order to ensure that the manipulation that you attempt to use is successful. These three criteria must all be met if you want to have the best possible chance at controlling those around you. If you really want to be successful, then, you must be able to conceal your intentions, understand the vulnerabilities of other people, and have the ruthlessness to do it all without feeling bad about it.

Concealing intentions

The first rule of manipulation is that you must be able to conceal your intentions. When it comes right down to it, if you make it clear to someone else that you are attempting to manipulate them, you lose all of the power that you need. If they know what you are doing, they are not going to fall for it just by virtue of the fact that they will know about it. When they are aware of what you are doing, they are not as likely to fall for it just because your attempts to get them to do something are no longer underhanded. If they know what you want them to do and they know that you are being vocal about it, you are no longer manipulating them—you are attempting to persuade them.

When it comes down to manipulation, then, you must be able to conceal your intentions. Think of it this way—imagine that you want your partner to do something for you. Perhaps you do not want to do the dishes that evening. You would rather sleep or play video games or do something else entirely. So, instead of getting up to do the dishes, you sigh and groan and grumble about getting up. You do not tell your partner that you do not want to do the dishes or ask your partner to do them for you. Rather, you attempt to get up, and without saying anything about it, you make it clear that you are not looking forward to moving or getting up in the first place.

When you do this, you show your partner how you feel. You are attempting to take advantage of your partner's empathy for you—you are hoping that, if your partner sees how unhappy or how uncomfortable you are, he or she will volunteer to help you instead. He or she will then want to help you feel better and therefore will likely volunteer to help you out, therefore allowing you to get precisely what you were looking for in the first place. Your partner thinks that they chose to help you because they cared and you are left happily basking in the benefits that you reaped all along just by knowing what was likely to pull at your partner's heartstrings along the way.

Understanding vulnerabilities

Next, you must be well aware of the vulnerabilities that the other person has if you hope to be able to control them. This makes sense—you cannot control someone else if you do not know how to get them to behave. We all have different vulnerabilities. Some of us are more prone to giving in to guilt. Others are prone to feeling highly empathetic toward others and therefore will help make people feel better through preying on that empathy that they do have. Others still may be too self-conscious to defend themselves when it comes down to being told that they should do something, and others are so desperate for attention that if you offer to give it to them, they will jump at the opportunity.

When you are able to figure out which kinds of vulnerabilities someone else has, then, you are able to take advantage of them entirely. You will be able to essentially discover what it is about someone else that you care to take advantage of, and in using that to your own added benefit, you can usually get pretty far with them. You may be able to convince them to do something because they feel like it is the only way that they can get what they want.

You may be able to get them to feel like what they are doing is only going to be beneficial and matter if they do things in a certain way. No matter what, however, if you can tap into a vulnerability that someone else has, you will begin to see their behaviors change. You will see the ways that they can change their behaviors and you will begin to develop that degree of control that you were looking for over them.

Ruthlessness

Finally, the last point that you must remember and the final criterion of manipulation that is to be successful is a degree of ruthlessness that you must develop. You need this ruthlessness if you hope to be able to influence or control what someone else is thinking or feeling. If you can control what they think or how they behave, you know that you are ultimately able to better take advantage of them. However, that control is only useful if you do not feel guilty about it.

Many people find that they cannot get over this—they feel like they cannot help but feel bad when they do something to someone else that they would not like done to themselves. Some people cannot bring themselves to attempt to take advantage of someone else, especially if the primary method of taking advantage of them in the first place is one that will be directly harmful to them. They may feel guilty about it and they may feel like they are doing something wrong. This will be directly incompatible with being able to manipulate someone else, however—if you are going to feel bad about what you are doing, you cannot hope to remain successful at it in the long run. You cannot hope to fully take advantage of other people if you know that you will feel guilty about it, especially if that guilt is likely to simply make you feel bad and tell the other person what you are doing.

It is only when you can step away from that guilt altogether and develop that cold ruthlessness to not care about what you are doing to other people that you will be able to really be successful.

Methods of Manipulation

When it comes down to how people manipulate others, there are countless methods that can be used. Some people make use of methods that involve lying. Others try using methods that rely on constant showering and inundation of love or affection. There are many different manners that people can be controlled in and there is no rule that you must use any one method in particular. However, each and every technique that you will see can typically be classified into one of five different categories. Some forms of manipulation are considered positive reinforcement while others are negative, and others still are partial. Some people rely on punishment and others still rely on some form of traumatic event to get someone else to change how they behave.

At the end of the day, being able to understand these five criteria will allow you to better see how the manipulation attempts that you will be learning about will work. You will see that they all vary greatly from type to type, but they are all successful in their own unique ways. We will be going over each and every type of rein-forcement within this section—we will be discovering what it means to use each of these types of reinforcement.

Positive reinforcement

Positive reinforcement is a behavioral reinforcement that is meant to make someone continue to perform what they have done. It involves preventing something that is desirable as the consequence for a behavior that was performed. Keep in mind that not all conse-quences are negative—a consequence is simply the result of the behavior or action that was taken and it can be positive, negative, or neutral.

When making use of positive reinforcement, you are going to be providing the individual that you are manipulating with a positive factor or a positive result when they perform the behavior that you want to see. Usually, you can see positive reinforcement as a praise or a reward for doing the right action at the right time. Think of this as providing an allowance for your children if they do all of their chores for the week. You want them to feel incentivized to perform the right behaviors so you will give them the rewards that they need to keep them interested in doing so.

This is done often in manipulation as well—you may use love bombing, for example. This is a method that is commonly done to encourage the other party to behave in a very specific way because they want to continue to be showered with love, gifts, and affection for doing so. If you want to make use of this, you simply need to figure out the positive reinforcement that you plan on using and you provide it every single time that the other person or party does what you want to encourage.

Negative reinforcement

Negative reinforcement is the opposite—it is reinforcing a behavior by the removal of something negative when it is done properly. For example, imagine that you work a job that says that, if you complete all of your weekly work, you can have an extra day off. The catch, however, is that you have to complete that extra work during the week prior to the day. If you finish your work by Thursday evening and have nothing left on your weekly to-do list, you are told that you can have the Friday off. In this instance, having to go in to work for that Friday shift would be the negative reinforcer. You would rather not work on Friday, so your production during the week has increased and improved so you can have an extra day off that week.

When it comes to manipulation, the negative reinforcer will oftentimes be something that you would least expect. It may be that you are told that you will not have to do as much work if you do what the manipulator wants. It could be that you offer to forgive something if the other person does something else for you in return. It is meant to essentially work by making sure that the other party feels like helping or giving in to what is expected is going to be better than not.

Partial reinforcement

Partial reinforcement is essentially inconsistent reinforcement. It is meant to create a feeling of doubt or insecurity that can be preyed upon. It makes the individual feel like winning or getting that positive result is an option, but they have to sort of take a risk to make it happen. It is meant to instill some doubt or uncertainty into the other person. Surprisingly enough, when the chances of reward is made to be unpredictable, the individual that is going to be trying to get that reward will likely chase it far more often than if someone who was used to regular positive reinforcement would if it simply stopped happening.

This is essentially playing upon those same methods that are used to trap gamblers into continuing to throw money toward their games that they play. They will repeatedly sink money into the gambling in hopes of winning because they know that they have to win at some point. After all, statistically speaking, they will at some point in time, so long as they keep playing, and the longer they go without being rewarded, the more they try because they believe that statistically, it will happen at some point soon.

Punishment

Punishment refers to the addition of something negative to the situation. You can add it to either the behavior being performed if you want that behavior to be ended, or you can use it until the behavior is performed until the punishment is ended. When you punish someone else, you are going to be making them uncomfortable or unhappy with the idea of repeatedly not following through with what needs to be done or what you would like for them to do. This can be done in many ways—some of them being more obvious than others. Punishments such as nagging or the silent treatment are two such examples. One continues to bother someone until the behavior is completed while the other refuses to speak to the other person until the behavior is completed.

When you use punishment, you want to make doing the opposite of what you want as unpleasant as possible so the other person decides to follow along with your wishes and gives in to you. When you do that, you ensure that you can get your way—you ensure that you more or less force the other person into wanting to give you what you wanted to make the punishment stop.

Trauma

Finally, the last method of attempting to manipulate someone else is through the use of trauma. Usually, these methods are the most overtly abusive of them all. Some of these will be through the use of verbal abuse. Others will make use of explosive tempers or attempting to intimidate the other person into obedience. Some will attempt to establish some degree of dominance or superiority over the other person and others will attempt to make the person being manipulated so incredibly wary about angering or frustrating the manipulator.

Essentially the manipulator is going to be trying to train the other person to avoid doing anything that would be deemed as contradictory or confrontational. The idea is to make the other person as afraid or intimidated by the idea of annoying or disagreeing with the manipulator as possible so the manipulator can continue to take advantage of the situation. The more that this happens, the more in control the manipulator gets to become, and with some of the most extreme methods of this form of manipulation, they only have to happen once before they become effective.

EMOTIONS AND MANIPULATION

ULTIMATELY, at the heart of most manipulation is the emotion behind it. Emotions are difficult for people to contradict—most of the time, when you feel something, you are driven to act by it. You feel like you have no choice but to follow through with it. You feel like you are compelled to act in certain ways—and most of the time, you are entirely unaware of this happening and how it works in the first place. Emotions are there for people to help guide them—they are very important to life and they are oftentimes used in all sorts of ways that are meant to be motivational.

However, it is the very way in which emotions work that makes them so readily available for manipulation in the first place. Emotions are oftentimes targeted to be manipulated because they are easy to control for other people when they know what they are doing and because people are able to influence and control these emotions, they are usually able to manipulate and control the other person as well.

· · ·

*W*ithin this chapter, we will seek to better understand emotions in general. We will be taking a closer look at what emotions are and how they tend to work for everyone involved. We will be looking at what they are and how they are able to motivate people to action. Finally, we will take a look at the steps necessary to control and manipulate the emotions of someone else.

*T*his chapter is important to understand, as ultimately, it is when you are able to take control of the emotions of other people that you are best able to take control of the people as well. It is very important that you are able to recognize how to control emotions first and understand how that control can be beneficial to you and getting your way.

Defining Emotions

Emotions, if you had to put a definition to them, would be an instinctive and reflexive state of mind. By this definition, they happen automatically, and the wayt hat they oftentimes happen is through the unconscious mind. You have two facets to your mind —the conscious aspect that is able to be directly influenced and controlled, and the unconscious mind, which exists on the outside of your awareness. These are both very powerful parts of your mind and they serve very different, albeit equally important, purpose.

*E*ssentially, your conscious mind is the part that you know about. Everything that you think, feel, and perceive is a part of your collective conscious mind—it is what you are actively aware of in that particular moment. At this point in time, your conscious mind is likely mostly preoccupied with reading the words in this book. The unconscious mind is always running in the background. It is keeping everything functioning in the background while your conscious mind is free to do what it needs to. This allows for your conscious mind to not have to deal so much with aspects that are not currently relevant, though they may become relevant in the future. Essentially, these processes are here so you do not have to worry about what is going on everywhere around you—your unconscious mind filters out what matters and what does not and then allows you to better process everything.

*W*hen you go back to emotions, then, your emotions are entirely unconscious. They happen without your input and without your bidding. Positive or not, they exist to change the way that you are going to respond to the world around you. They are there to guide your behaviors directly, which we will get to in just a moment. Essentially, then, your mind will automatically process what it sees around you and then reflexively respond to what has been processed by creating an emotion. This is essentially the only real way that your unconscious mind can respond to the world around you. It cannot respond directly—it has to influence you to behave.

*G*enerally speaking, there are six emotions that are believed to be the most basic emotions of all. These six emotions are the six that people everywhere will feel and respond with. They are the emotions that create the foundation for everything else that people feel. These six emotions are:

- **Happiness:** This emotion is designed to reward you for something. Essentially, something that you did was deemed to be beneficial for you or good for you to continue doing in the future, so your body and mind reward you for it. They make you feel like what you did was worth repeating with happiness. Happiness comes from behaviors that are designed to be encouraging of your continued survival and propagation. For example, eating good foods, exercising, and sexual acts can all lead to increases in happiness thanks to the fact that all three of those will directly contribute to the continued thriving of yourself and your genetic material.

- **Sadness:** Sadness is like the opposite of happiness. When it comes to sadness, you feel it to try to discourage repetition of the behavior that you were engaging in. You are essentially recognizing that the behavior that you were engaging in is actually harmful in some way, so you feel sad, typically in response to some sort of loss. This is meant to prevent you from ever repeating those behaviors again—when you know that they led to you feeling incredibly sad, you feel like the repetition of those behaviors is likely to be a major problem.

- **Anger:** Anger is meant to encourage a fight response when you have been threatened or otherwise felt like you were in danger. It is meant to make you ready to defend yourself if necessary if you feel like you may be harmed if you do not. Anger is one of those emotions that is commonly misunderstood—people oftentimes assume that it is a problematic behavior and emotion when in reality, it serves a very important purpose that should not be avoided out of fear of it getting out of hand.

- **Fear:** Fear is the other side of anger—when you feel fear, you are oftentimes responding to being threatened.

Typically, fear actually comes first. You feel fear when you are threatened, and that fear can turn into anger if your unconscious mind thinks that you can fight off the threat. Your fear is there to help you stay alive—it leads to your body to feel more alert and aware of everything going on around you to be able to snap to defense if necessary.

- **Surprise:** Surprise is something that you will feel if something does not look quite right. Typically, surprise is there for you to feel when you realize that something is not meshing with what it should have. Something may seem out of place and therefore need more attention to parse out what it means or how this will influence your attempts to respond.

- **Disgust:** Finally, disgust is a feeling that you are around something that is going to be dangerous to your health, physically or mentally. Typically, the most standardized source of disgust that people have is when they feel it toward something that is rotting or otherwise toxic.

Emotions as Motivators

Ultimately, the emotions that you feel are strongly motivating. They are there for a very important reason—to allow you to respond to the world around you. They are there to allow your unconscious mind to be able to directly communicate with your body. They are there to make you feel that need to act in a certain way. Most of the time, when it comes to your emotions, you will find that you feel like you must do things in a very specific way. You may feel angry and therefore feel like you are ready to punch someone in the face. You may feel sad and feel like you want nothing more than to retreat to lick your proverbial wounds and get away from everyone around you.

· · ·

*N*o matter the way that you respond to your emotions, however, they work this way for one particular reason: Your emotions are designed to influence your behaviors. This is primarily because, at the end of the day, everything that you do, feel and think, are all intimately related to each other. Your thoughts that you have are very powerful in this instance—the thoughts that you have will always color your emotions that you have. Think about it this way—if you have negative thoughts about dogs because you suffered a dog bite when you were a child, of course you will feel negatively when you see a dog go by. This is only natural—the sight of the dog walking past you becomes colored by the thought that you had. Your feelings toward the dog are likely fear and they are likely directly attributed to that initial thought.

*W*hen you feel fear, then, your body responds accordingly. You find that your pulse increases. Your breathing picks up. You feel powerful and ready to run at a moment's notice, should you have to do so. You feel this way primarily because you think that you may need to run away. You feel like this because you know that you need to fight off any threats that come your way, or you will need to escape. You have associated the sight of a dog with a dangerous situation, so your body responds accordingly.

*T*his is important to keep in mind—when you want to control people, then, you will find that the easiest way to do so is through controlling emotions, and for the most part, the easiest way that you can control the amounts of someone else is through directly targeting their thoughts.

Manipulating Emotions

Emotions, because they are unconscious and because they are so motivating, are actually surprisingly easy to manipulate. Thanks to the fact that they are unconscious, many people may not realize why they are feeling the way that they are. They may not recognize the initial source of their discomfort or stress. They may not understand what it is that is stressing them out. They may not see what matters at the end of the day and they may be easily controlled thanks to this fact. However, because so many people are entirely out of touch with that connection between thoughts and feelings, they are highly easy to control. When you decide that you want to manipulate emotions, there is not much to it. At the end of the day, you will need to meet a few simple steps, but if you can do that, you will find that the manipulation process becomes incredibly simple.

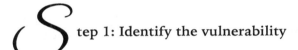 tep 1: Identify the vulnerability

o begin, you must discover what the other person's vulnerability that you would like to control is. You are going to be looking for what it is that drives the other person that you can take control of. You are looking for the ways that you can control the other person to figure out how you are most likely to succeed. This can be the hardest step a lot of the time, especially if you do not really know the person that you are attempting to manipulate yet. For example, imagine that you are a salesperson trying to land a sale. Chances are, you do not have very much time at all to figure out what it is that motivates the other person or how you can control them. This is not a failure on your part— rather, it is the simple reality of the job and how it works.

. . .

*W*hen you work this job, however, you are going to need to get good at identifying these weaknesses that can be controlled quickly and easily. The easiest ones to look for are dependent upon the individual—are you talking to someone who has young kids? Usually, you can rely on those new parent fears to really help push them through to doing what you want them to do. Are they easily controlled by someone being more intelligent than them? Establish yourself as an authority figure.

*S*tep 2: Trigger the emotion

*O*nce you know what the vulnerability is that you will be utilizing, it is time to trigger the emotion. You may be able to do this by talking to someone. You may use implications about what they are doing or what you think to try to instill doubt in the other person. No matter how you act, however, one thing holds true—in triggering the emotion, you should be able to then begin to influence their behaviors.

*S*tep 3: Manipulate

*W*hen the emotion is triggered, you should see the individual begin to act in the way that you were looking for them to. If you can see that they change their behaviors, you can then begin to reinforce the actions. You can continue to trigger the emotion to continue to benefit from it being there in the first place and in doing so, you should be able to maintain your control over the other person.

HOW MANIPULATION WORKS

ULTIMATELY, manipulation works because it takes control of two very important motivators. It takes advantage of exploiting vulnerabilities that people have, most of the time which will trigger emotional reactions, and it take advantage of needs that people have. Most manipulation winds up being successful because it can check off one of those boxes. When it is able to exploit a need or a vulnerability, it is able to better manage the reactions necessary. After all, people are surprisingly predictable in their responses to the world and if you can figure out the right needs or vulnerabilities to exploit, you are likely to get precisely what you are looking for.

Within this chapter, we are going to take a look at these various needs and vulnerabilities. Keep in mind as you read through this chapter that this is not a comprehensive list—there are others that exist. However, these are the most common ones that you are likely to encounter.

Vulnerabilities to Exploit

People everywhere have all sorts of vulnerabilities that they have. These are vulnerabilities that will make someone much more susceptible to manipulation. If you are looking to manipulate someone else, these are the most common signs that you will want to look for. These are the signs that will let you know that this individual is likely to be readily and easily exploitable and controllable.

A desire to please

*W*hile it is only natural to want to make other people happy, some people take it too far. They find that they cannot function if they are not taking responsibility for the happiness of everyone around them. Rather than helping other people, they allow themselves to do anything that they possibly can, no matter the cost, to ensure that the people around them are going to be taken care of. They oftentimes will do anything in their power to ensure that they please other people, even if they do so at their own cost or their own detriment. They may feel like the only real value that they have is in their own ability to please other people and they act upon it. They need to feel like they are making other people feel happy to feel like they can justify their own self-worth.

A fear of negative emotions

. . .

*A*nother common vulnerability is the fear of negative emotions. Some people find that they cannot deal with people that are strongly negative. They feel like they cannot cope with the presence of those negative emotions all around them and as a direct result, they usually find that they would rather walk on eggshells and give everyone around them what they want rather than attempting to do what they can or what they should do. They would rather make the wrong choice if it meant that they would not have to deal with the repercussions of negative emotions all around them. They would much rather feel like they were able to avoid the negativity than anything else.

A lack of assertiveness

*S*ome people are vulnerable because they simply cannot say no. Every time that they try to stand up for themselves, they find that they are stuck fighting with themselves over it. They find that there is no easy or clear-cut way for them to say no. Sometimes, they feel too afraid of the results to resist, and other times, they are simply too self-conscious or they lack the confidence necessary to stand up for themselves. They would rather take the negativity on than anything else and they would rather be the ones to suffer than to try standing up to someone else.

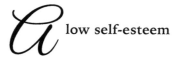 low self-esteem

. . .

*S*ome people are easy to control because they do not trust themselves at all. They have a low self-esteem, perhaps because of a childhood or a lifetime of struggling, or perhaps related to some other reason. Nevertheless, they feel like they cannot stand up for themselves and as a direct result, they are easily exploited. Their lack in trust of themselves leads to them doubting and second-guessing every decision that they make simply because they do not feel like they can make good ones. Instead of trying, they simply defer to other people because they assume that other people will get it right. Of course, this means that they can be easily manipulated without very much effort at all.

A lack of boundaries

*W*hen people lack boundaries, they can usually be steamrolled into compliance. Think of it this way— when you lack boundaries, you are lacking the necessary protection to fight off attempts to manipulate. When you lack boundaries, you may see nothing wrong with someone else attempting to control you in some way, shape, or form. It may seem entirely acceptable or understandable for someone to tell you that you are messing up or tell you that you should behave differently because you do not have a boundary against it in the first place. Similarly speaking, you may find that you are easily or readily controlled because you do not feel like you have or deserve a certain standard of respect or treatment.

· · ·

Naiveté

When you are naïve, it can be difficult to rationalize that some people are simply cruel or deceptive. This, however, means that you are easily manipulated. People that are naïve usually take the world and the way that people act at face value. They assume that everything is readily explained away or understood as being exactly what they are told. However, this means that they are very easy to take advantage of.

The benefit of the doubt

Some people are unwilling to recognize that badness exists. They are entirely resistant to the idea that they may be giving other people the benefit of the doubt when it should not be given. They are willing to explain away being wronged, over and over again, and as a direct result, they are oftentimes willing to accept whatever it is that the manipulator says. They would rather take the manipulator at face value and give them the benefit of the doubt than feel like they were to untrusting or judgmental toward the manipulator. Of course, this means that they are quite easy to take advantage of as a direct result.

A lack of self-confidence

. . .

*W*hen you lack confidence, you are someone that is going to struggle with being able to see that you may have been right at some point in time. When you lack confidence, you feel like, at the end of the day, you are wrong if someone else tells you that you are. You would rather believe that you were wrong than attempt to defend yourself—usually because you think of yourself as worthless or useless. Of course, this means that you are very easy to manipulate as well. When you are easy to control or manipulate, you are at an increased risk of being targeted.

*O*verthinking

*S*ome people tend to err on the side of overthinking things. This is usually in line with the overly conscientious attitude that people have when they give manipulators the benefit of the doubt. The victim, when they overthink, spend too much time trying to understand the reason behind the manipulation. They are trying to rationalize it away as not actually being that bad or not actually being a problem because they do not see it as a problem. However, it is a very real problem—and when they refuse to acknowledge that, they set themselves as very easy to control.

A submissive personality type

• • •

*F*inally, the last vulnerability that we are going to discuss that will make someone highly susceptible to manipulation is being a naturally submissive person. Some people simply are submissive—they do not see a reason to resist or a reason that they should be trying to better avoid the situation around them. They find that it is easier to be manipulated and be dependent upon the manipulator for some reason. Some are simply codependent—they only feel worthy or valuable if they are actively enabling someone else. Others are simply likely to struggle with not feeling valued or feeling unimportant. No matter the reason, however, submissive people are much easier to exploit than those that are dominant or those that are likely to feel like they can better fight off a threat.

Needs to Exploit

At the end of the day, all of these vulnerabilities are usually joined by one of two needs—the need to be right and the need to be accepted. People have these two deep-seeded needs that are the reason that they are so likely to give in to any sort of attempt to manipulate them in the first place. It is only when one of these two needs come into play that people are actually able to be controlled and influenced. These are the two needs that drive forward any sort of social influence. They are what keep people motivated to change and they drive people to act in ways that they may not actually be genuinely comfortable with. However, they hold onto this notion that they need to change up what they are doing to better cope. They change to be right or they change to be liked.

The need to be right

· · ·

$\mathcal{T}$he need to be right is referred to as the informational social influence. This is the natural desire that people have to be right at all times. Think about it—when you argue with someone, why does it get so heated? Typically, it is because both sides see the other person as being in the wrong. Both people feel like the other person is entirely wrong and therefore, entirely out of line. This is important to remember—when you feel like you are in the wrong, you are naturally going to want to comply. You are going to want to shift to being right somehow, and oftentimes the way that you can do so is through figuring out how to align your-self, your behaviors, and even your beliefs in some instances, to fit within that paradigm of being right.

$\mathcal{T}$his is a very common one—people will give into this when they are presented with the evidence that shows that they are actually in the wrong. When you see that other people are all saying that you are wrong and that you need to change up your behaviors to fit in with them, you are likely to do so. You do not want to be wrong—being wrong is embarrassing. This particular form of influence is usually attained through making it clear to the other party that they need to accept what is being said. It involves providing someone with clear enough evidence to accept that your method of seeing the world is the right one that they are willing to comply. It usually leads to complete acceptance—when people recognize that someone else is right, there is usually a shift in both acting as demanded and also thinking as demanded.

· · ·

The need to be liked or accepted

The second need is a bit more nuanced. At the end of the day, we all want to be liked. We all naturally crave being liked and accepted because we are a social species. There is no way around it—we love other people and we love other animals. We want to be a part of the in crowd at all costs and we will do just about anything in our power to make sure that we are.

However, that drive to be liked, that drive for normative value, is so influential on our behaviors that it becomes a very easy mode of manipulation. Think about it—people are constantly trying to comply with societal or peer pressure. Even when you get out of high school, there is some degree of societal pressure that is always there. You are expected to go out, get a job, and work to buy a house and start a family. This is simply expected of people and those that do not comply often feel like they need to explain themselves for their lack of compliance. When you look around, you can see that there is a very clear pattern of fashion trends as well that people tend to follow. These fashion trends are another way in which you can see that people will simply give in to the world around them.

Of course, this leads them wide open to manipulation in general. It becomes very easy to get in there and convince someone that they have to do something in order to be liked or in order to be valued. This appeal to societal pressure usually leads to some degree of compliance—you see this in high school when a student that has been so resistant for so long suddenly tries marijuana for the first time because their peers are pressuring them. You see it when a young adult gets pressured into going to a party that they do not want to go to, or when someone at work is told that they have to do something or risk losing their jobs. Peer pressure comes into play and influences others. As social animals, we want to be liked. We want to be accepted. We want to be desired and appreciated so much that we are willing to give up our own values to attain it.

METHODS OF EMOTIONAL
MANIPULATION

Now, with all of the important background information out of the way, it is time to start taking a look at the ways in which manipulation can be used. Within this chapter, we are going to be spending time in particular looking at methods of emotional manipulation. You will firstly be guided through understanding what emotional manipulation is. Then, you will be shown five distinct forms of manipulation that people can use to control the emotions of other people—you will see what they are and the steps to making them work for you to understand how they can be used.

What is Emotional Manipulation?

Emotional manipulation is using the emotions of someone else to allow for the exercise of control or influence over them. It is taking control of the individual's emotions and attempting to use those emotions in any way necessary to ensure that, at the end of the day, they are compliant with what you want them to do. It is important to recognize that this is most often done through making people feel uncertain or negatively about themselves in hopes of taking control of them later on. It is meant to allow you to ensure that you see the results that you want—as soon as you want them.

*W*hen you take a look at emotional manipulation, you are going to be spending time understanding that you are playing inside the mind of someone else. You are attempting to use mind games in order to really get that necessary control over someone else. You are creating an emotion in some way and then letting that emotion take its toll however necessary.

*W*ithin this chapter, we will see five distinct methods of doing so, though there are many others as well. You will see how you can use gaslighting, minimizing, devaluation, playing the victim, and love bombing to take control of someone else to get them to do whatever it is that you are hoping that they will.

Gaslighting

Of all of the methods that you will see within this book, gaslighting is perhaps the most insidious of them all. Making use of gaslighting allows you to take control of the mind of someone else. It is designed to encourage the other person to not trust themselves. It is meant to create someone who feels so doubtful in themselves and their own mind that they would rather trust you because they trust you more than they trust themselves. You are essentially making them doubt that they can properly perceive the world around them. You are teaching them that, at the end of the day, they cannot trust themselves or their mind. They cannot trust their senses and they cannot trust their beliefs or even their memories.

. . .

This method takes time to develop, but at the end of the day, it is perhaps one of the most powerful that you can use if your goal is to ensure that the other person feels dependent upon you or if you want them to rely on you in any way. However, keep in mind that with this method, you are essentially destroying a person's thought processes. You are degrading their trust and rendering them a shell of the person that they used to be.

Step 1: Trust

To begin this process, you need trust. You need to ensure that the person that you are attempting to manipulate sees you as entirely trustworthy and therefore someone that can be respected and believed to be doing the right thing. This oftentimes takes time—you need to ensure that you establish yourself as reliable and trustworthy for them. Usually, this means that you must develop the proper sort of relationship with them. You want to be dependable. You want to ensure that people around you are trusting of you. You want to ensure that, in particular, the person that you are trying to manipulate trusts you. IN particular, you will want to make sure that they genuinely like you. You want to excite them. You want to make them love you. You want them to not only trust you, but also love you because then they are willing to put up with so much more than they would need to.

Step 2: Create a catalog of mistakes

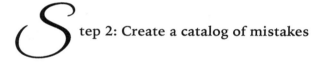

$\mathcal{U}$sually, step 2 happens alongside step 1. As you are bettering your relationship, you will want to ensure that you are constantly noting each and every mistake that the other person makes. You are wanting to ensure that, no matter what happens, you can say that they have messed up before and therefore cannot trust themselves. This step is relatively simple—after all, we make mistakes regularly. People make mistakes sometimes, but not all of the time. However, if you wish to gaslight someone, you need them to feel like they are constantly making mistakes so they are more likely to listen to you. Every time that the other person begins to doubt what is going on, it is your job to step in and point out how they are making a major mistake. At some point along the way, the target will eventually agree that they were wrong. They will see that they have been wrong so much in the past that there is no clear way that they can properly accept being right later on.

$\mathcal{S}$tep 3: The misunderstanding

$\mathcal{N}$ext, after making it clear to the other person that they are wrong, you must make sure that you also establish that you are not able to understand what they are talking about. Even if what they are saying is as logical as $2+2=4$, you must act as if what they are saying makes no sense at all. You must be willing and able to see that what they are saying is entirely false or wrong. You want to tel them that their own interpretation is entirely wrong, and then provide them with the correct answer— the one that you need them to have—while also stating it as if it is simple. Essentially, you would want to convincingly tell the other person that 2+2=5 even though you know that is not actually true in any real way, shape or form.

Step 4: Forgetting

Continuing on with the process, you will need to start tearing down what they say that they have done. You want them to start to doubt their memory. Essentially, if they say that they have done something minor or small, you can tell them that they are wrong. If you insist enough about something that is more or less irrelevant, such as whether their keys were on the desk, the counter, or hung up by the door, they will usually agree with you. They will believe that you are right about what you are saying. With enough repeated exposure to this process, they will eventually agree that you are right and they will stop trusting whether or not they can remember something. They will readily accept what you are saying any time that you say it.

Step 5: Downplaying

Finally, the last step that you will need to follow through with is to ensure that you trivialize anything that is said. If the target begins to voice any concerns about their memory or their mental state, or if they attempt to tell you that they believe that you may be lying to them, your job is to dismiss and downplay it. This is necessary to allow you to continue to make use of these methods—when you can downplay what is happening around you, you can usually begin to see them accepting what you have to say. You can usually get them to agree that you are right or that they should not be very concerned.

*R*emember, the entire purpose here when you gaslight someone else is to make them doubt themselves. You want them to resist their own feelings in favor of your own. You want them to rely on you as their only real source of reality. They will trust that you will provide that for them—they will assume that you will not be trying to hurt them because the idea of someone being disingenuous is that appalling to them. They will assume that you are being honest the entire time and that assumption will render them vulnerable for a longer period of time.

Minimizing

Another form of emotional manipulation is minimization. When you minimize someone else's concerns, you are trying to make it seem like whatever has happened is not actually a cause for concern. You are trying to make it seem like whatever has happened is actually much smaller than it actually was. This is usually done to avoid trouble or to sort of discredit the individual that may be voicing a concern or trying to resist what is going on around them. When you minimize someone else, you are going to need to make use of two distinct parts. These two parts come together to create the event of being minimized in the first place.

enial

. . .

*T*he first part of minimizing something is denial. When you deny that something is as bad as the other person is making it out to e, you are essentially making further use out of gaslighting. You are telling them that things were nowhere near as bad as they thought. Usually, you can see this in attempting to downplay the feelings of guilt or of being hurt. You want to down-play so you can be certain that, at the end of the day, you are better off able to keep control of the situation.

*F*or example, imagine that your target is telling you that they are very frustrated because you are always waving them away or that you are never present when they need you. Rather than accepting that, however, you would be telling them that in reality, they are being too sensitive. You tell them that they are reading into things too much. You tell them that they are wrong to feel that way.

*R*ationalization

*A*t the same time, you must also rationalize what is actually happening. You try to offer up a reason for what is happening that is just reasonable enough that they would seem crazy to disagree. This is essentially finding a degree of plausible deniability. This is essentially using an excuse that cannot realisti-cally or rationally be argued against. For example, imagine that you tell the target, after they have complained that you are not present enough emotionally, that you are not actually avoiding them or that you are not actually attempting to neglect them, but you have been very busy with work and you have had a lot on your mind. You cannot really argue with that—if your target is not actually present when you are at work, they would likely have no idea what the true workload or strain is. They cannot argue and tell you that you cannot spend time working—that is irrational. This leaves them feeling discredited and like they have no right to be upset.

Devaluation

Devaluation is another common form of emotional manipulation that can be used. This one is designed to make the other person feel like they are not as valuable to you. It is meant to be used in tandem with intermittent reinforcement—the idea is that when you start to lose interest in the target, they will feel the pressure to become more desirable. They will do whatever they can to maintain your affection, even if they are doing so in ways that are not particularly in line with their own values. They will jump to try to get you back in line because they are afraid that you will reject them entirely.

This is really done primarily just by pulling back over time. If you are using this on a romantic partner or a friend, the best way to do so is to slowly but surely let them go. You stop relying on them. You stop reaching out on your own as often. You do not shower them with the affection that you may have done in the past.

Playing the Victim

Playing the victim is another common method that can be used to control other people. When you are going to make use of playing the victim, you are essentially turning the tables. This is primarily used when you feel like the target is starting to piece together that you have been manipulating them. This happens when you begin to feel like your attempts to manipulate are being questioned or are at risk of being discovered. This is done to essentially twist things around in a way that will put the target on the defensive, therefore eliminating those attempts to expose the true manipulation where it is occurring.

*T*his particular method exists in three stages that must be followed. It does not take long to use this method and if you play your cards just right, you will essentially turn things around so the target is so busy worrying about proving you wrong that they stop their onslaught of trying to prove to you that you are wrong. These three stages are deny, attack, and reverse victim and offender. You can remember this with the acronym, DARVO.

 eny

*T*he first step to this process is to deny what is happening. You do not want the other person to be able to say that you did not deny what was said. You must say that you are not manipulating anyone or deny any claims that the other person has said. For example, if your target has said that you are manipulative, you must tell them that they are entirely wrong. You tell them that you are not a manipulative person and then move on to the next step.

 ttack

· · ·

*N*ext, you move to the attack step. This step is all about turning tables. Here, you must point out that, in reality, you are not actually the one that is manipulative. You then point out that your target is actually an abuser and that you hate that you have no choice but to put up with it. The entire point here is to switch things around. You are defending yourself by attacking back, and this is typically highly effective. You may also pair this with a method of also attacking the other person in some other way. You may say that you are going to break up with the target, or you may threaten some consequence—you could, for example, say that you will not tolerate such defamation or threaten to sue.

Reverse victim and offender

*F*inally, you must turn things around here. You are suddenly the victim at this point in time. You make it clear that you are truly suffering at the hands and abuse of the other person. You may point out all of the ways in which the other person is destroying your life. You may say that you feel like you are walking on eggshells or that you feel like you cannot possibly cope with things the way that they are. You may cry or attempt to make things sound worse than they actually are. The whole point here is to make yourself seem like you are in worse condition than the target—and it has to be at the fault of the target.

Love Bombing

The last form of emotional manipulation that we are going to take a look at is love bombing. This one is incredibly simple and does not require a step-by-step guide. All you will do during this step is attempt to convince the other person that they should love you. You are trying to convince them that, at the end of the day, you are associated with good feelings. Most commonly, you can achieve this by associating yourself with the endorphin rush of giving gifts or giving love.

*E*ssentially, you want to addict the target to you through the generous gift giving that you will use. You will tell the other person how special they are. You will encourage them to feel like they are the best person you know. You will place them on a pedestal and shower them with lavish gifts or trips that are inappropriate given the circumstances. The idea here is that you want the other person to feel as special as possible so you can keep them reliant on you as long as possible. You want them to feel like they want to keep you around. You want them to feel like, at the end of the day, they are lucky to have you because you make it clear to them that you are associated with good feelings.

*T*his is oftentimes compared to the first stage in the cycle of abuse—the honeymoon period. You want to do whatever you can here to make the target feel like they really, truly matter to you. You want the target to feel valued entirely. You want them to feel happy and excited when you are around. This is essentially allowing you to build up the trust and love that you will need to use other methods of manipulation later on. You want them to be happy and accepting of everything so you know that, at the end of the day, they are going to want to continue to associate with you. You want them to always want to be around you, and the best way to do that is to show them this idealized, perfect version of yourself that will become an addiction for them. As soon as they are addicted to you and thoroughly attached, however, you can begin to let this slip away, little by little.

Typically, this method is paired with devaluation. When they are paired together, you can create a cycle between the two that essentially encourages the other person to do anything possible to keep you around. They will work as hard as they can to keep you around because they have deemed you to be valuable and desirable.

METHODS OF MIND CONTROL

HAVE YOU EVER WISHED THAT, at the end of the day, you could control minds? Has there ever been a time where you have looked at someone and felt that things would be so much easier and so much better if you could simply control what they thought, how they thought it, and why they did what they did? You may wish that you could put a thought controller in their minds; you may wish that you could better influence those around you.

he truth is, you can do so. You can control the way in which people think and what they do. It may not be exact, as nothing gin life ever is, but the truth is, you can control anyone with ease. You can learn to control what people think, how they do it, and more. You can learn to better recognize the ways that your actions influence other people, and in learning to know how your actions impact everyone around you, you can become capable of great things. You can influence people around you to believe what you believe. You can subtly squeeze at their minds, pushing out outside influences until, at the end of the day, you can be the one in complete control.

*W*ithin this chapter, we are going to dive into the methods of using mind control. We will be looking at the ways in which you are able to ensure that, at the end of the day, you are in control. Being able to control what other people are doing becomes a way in which you can influence heavily. You can slowly craft their mind, molding it into precisely what you what. Little by little, bit by bit, you are able to manage the way that the other person sees the world and in doing so, you can better control everything.

*W*e are going to look at four methods of mind control. We will look at isolation as a form of mind control. Then, we will be looking at how you can use criticism to help yourself to control the thought processes of other people as well, instilling doubt and uncertainty and allowing you to control what they are thinking. You will discover the use of peer pressure, looking at the way in which, if you can manage the reactions of everyone around the one person that you are attempting to control, you can also manage to control the individual target. Finally, you will see the ways in which you can use repetition to slowly and carefully introduce a thought, allowing you to better take control of everything.

*E*ach of these methods that you are being provided will have their own very real, very different methods of utilization. They all allow you to better control the thoughts of everyone around you. However, at the center of all of them is trust.

You must be able to develop the trust that you will need in order to get that access to the other person's mind. The mind is one of the more protected aspect of the person, and while it is easy to control and influence it if you know what you are doing, the truth is, you need trust to make it happen. You need to be in a position of trust to know that what you are doing is right. It is only in that position of trust that you will get that power. It is only when you can be sure that you know what you are doing that you can really tap into the potential of other people's mind.

What is Mind Control?

Mind control is not what most people may initially think; it is not simply implanting a chip or some sort of spell or anything else in an attempt to be able to influence the way that other people see. It is not being able to perfectly control every aspect of everything going on. You do not get the power that you would grant you that perfect control over someone else. You do not get the ability to be able to ensure that, at the end of the day, you are able to control everything. You cannot perfectly tell someone to move exactly how you want. You must be able to control other people, rather, through the use of other methods.

There is no magic way that you can control someone like a robot. You cannot simply use a controller to slowly and carefully micromanage what is going on. However, what you can do is change the programming. Mind control, in the sense that you are seeing it here, is meant to help you to better control everything. It is meant to grant you the power to put in new programming. When it comes right down to it, mental programming is a more accurate way of looking at the most inherent functions.

*Y*ou are controlling the mind to control the behaviors. When it comes right down to it, we are all a slave to one simple way of life: The thoughts that we have control the way that we feel, and it is those feelings, those motivators that we have naturally, that influence the way in which we act. This constant loop between thoughts, feelings, and behaviors is never-ending. This cycle is there to make the way of functioning easier than ever. It allows your body and mind to take sorts of shortcuts so you do not have to figure out how better you can influence the way that you behave, allowing for more efficiency in the actions that you have that require you to pay closer attention.

*H*owever, because the body and mind work in tandem constantly, they become incredibly easy to take advantage of. It does not take very much effort to be able to completely control the way someone else behaves. All you have to do is implant your own thoughts into their mind. When they start to believe your thoughts, they will behave the way that you are hoping to get. Essentially, the more that you control the thoughts, the more that you get to control the ways that other people behave.

Isolation

The first method of control is isolation. Think about it—when people are isolated, they start to suffer. We are inherently social beings; we crave that social intimacy more than anything else. When you isolate someone else, you take control of their mind. In fact, when it comes down to it, many different cults make use of this method—to control other people, they work hard to isolate the members of the cult. When people become isolated, they start feeling like they have no choice but to stay. They are easier to wear down over time if they are cut off from everyone else. They start to doubt themselves, especially when they are also joined by the use of other methods of manipulation such as gaslighting to constantly fill the individual with doubt.

To isolate people, you must slowly but surely develop a relationship with them. You need to be in a position of trust, and to do that, you need some way to be in either a position of being trusted or a position of being in control. You can essentially take the time to get yourself there through the use of other methods—you can make use of the principles of persuasion to put yourself into an authority role. You can use the body language to influence the thoughts of other people. You can make use of mirroring, which we will be introducing shortly within this book in Chapter 8: Neuro-Linguistic Programming.

When you are in a position of trust, it becomes time for you to begin systematically forcing your point. It becomes time for you to begin, little by little, planting your thoughts. To isolate someone else, you must be able to carefully and quietly begin to convince them that no one else matters. You slowly put rifts between them and those around them. You work to ensure that you can remove that sense of connectedness between your target and those around you.

As you work to build your own relationship with the other person, you slowly persuade the other person to begin to adapt your own way of seeing the world. You carefully begin to talk to them, planting the seeds of an idea within them. You teach them what it is that you want them to believe, through many of the other ideas. Isolation is, in many ways, the first step that you must take in order to control minds. Once you get the other person isolated, you become the only person that they interact with. You are able to insert yourself into that position of trusted individual and it becomes an "us vs the world" mentality in which you are able to convince them that you have their best interest at heart and that you are desperately trying to take control of the situation. When they trust you and they trust that you mean it when you say that you are going to be helping them and that you do care about them, they let their guard down.

*I*t is when those defenses drop, when the individual stops worrying so much about whether you may or may not be a threat, that you are finally able to get in and change their thoughts. There are many different ways that you can choose to do so. You can choose to make yourself in that trusted position and then constantly change the way that you are interacting with the other person, changing their mind by repeating the point that you want them to. You could offer gentle, subtle criticisms in hopes that they will internalize them and live by them, allowing yourself to better deal with the problem at hand. It could be that you take the time to show them that they need to do what you are doing to fit in with you, making use of peer pressure. No matter the method that you choose to use, however, one thing is true: Your position of trust and your position as the only one in that position of trust, is what will help you. When you can develop that position of trust that will grant you that power, you are then the only one whose voice matters because yours is the only one that is heard.

. . .

*I*solation commonly is found to be in several different forms that vary greatly from type to type. Some of these types include:

- **Physical isolation:** This is the restriction of movement—you try to keep people closer to yourself without allowing them access to those external resources and influences that would otherwise become a distraction. It could be that you take someone on a weekend getaway, or you try to keep someone at your home. It does not have to be genuinely restricting someone; it could even be monopolizing time as well. It is trying to create that physical distance between the individual and everyone else.

- **Mental isolation:** When you isolate someone mentally, you make them *feel* alone. They may or may not actually be alone, but you set up so you are able to take total control of them. The longer that they are kept alone and isolated from people, such as through blocking phone communication or intercepting letters, the more likely you are to be able to control the other person's mind. The longer you keep them alone and isolated, or feeling like no one else cares, the more uncertain they become.

- **Censorship:** Another way, especially in cults in particular, that isolation can be used is through censorship. If you can get someone physically isolated and into a position in which they have no access to the media, no access to what is going on in the world, and no access to any other way to see the world, you are able to begin controlling the thoughts of the individual. You could only show them, for example, the messages that you know will help push your point. The more that you do this, and the more time goes by without them getting any sort of contradicting information, the more information that you can control.

Criticism

Criticism is an attempt to sort of control everything that is going on around you. When you criticize other people, you are able to slowly and surely grind them down. You are able to essentially force the point, making it so that you are better able to control them. You make them feel like they are the problem—they feel like they were the one that needed to change.

*W*hen you criticize someone else, you plant doubt. It can be subtle—and the best examples often are— where you quietly make a comment that can be hidden beyond a layer of plausible deniability. When you make use of criticism, you must first identify what it is that the other person is self-conscious about. You must be able to figure out what it is that they will most likely feel nervous about. You need to figure out what that aspect of themselves is so you can then begin to take advantage. You must be able to essentially grind away at that one chip, little by little.

*F*or example, imagine that you are trying to get your partner to do something. Perhaps you want them to lose weight. Or maybe you want them to go back to school to do something with themselves, or to get a job or do literally anything with themselves. You want them to try to actually do something with themselves so you can then expect them to better interact with the people around them. You want them to be able to do anything at all with themselves, but they do not seem to be interested in doing so.

. . .

*I*n this instance, all you have to do to plant that idea in their mind is to make them subtly begin to doubt themselves. You want to essentially plant the idea in their mind that they *can* do better. You want them to see that what they are currently doing is a problem for them. You want them to feel like they have no choice but to fix the problem in some way, shape, or form, so you can know that they are more likely to behave in the way that you prefer. The more that you can do with that, the better.

*F*or example, perhaps you subtly mention that you feel like people that are not educated are just being lazy, if your goal here is to get your partner to go to school. You slowly and subtly tear down the idea that you are trying to change in the other person's mind. Over time, you are able to wear them down. Over time, they start to feel a little bit insecure over what is going on. Over time, they will begin to feel doubtful in themselves. Over time, the criticism will make them feel like they need to work harder to get noticed, like they need to work harder to ensure that, at the end of the day, they do succeed. They will then do that work in hopes of alleviating that criticism, and you will have gotten that end result that you were looking for.

*W*hen you do this, you are effectively using shame. You are making the other person feel bad about themselves. You are attempting to get them to let go of something that makes them problematic in hopes of changing their behaviors, and if you did so effectively, you will notice that you do, in fact, see those changes that you were looking for. You will see the other person begin vying for any sort of affection or attention, positive or otherwise, and as they do so, you will notice that they are more likely to do what you want.

Peer Pressure

Peer pressure becomes another valid way in which you can better control people around you as well. When you want to control the mind of someone else, the best way to do so is to ensure that you can surround them with other people that are engaged those behaviors that you want to push. The more that you are able to better show the individual that everyone else is doing something, the more pressure that they will feel to comply. This sort of compliance is critically important to remember. When you make use of that kind of pressure, you are usually able to convince those around you that they should, in fact, make those changes that you need to see.

$\mathcal{T}$hink of the way that teenagers are so quick to do what they are told or asked to do because they want to fit in. They want to be liked. They want to be treated with fairness and respect. They want to feel like they belong with the people that they are interacting with. This is essential to them—they feel that need and they will work very hard to make it happen for themselves. They will think that the only way that they can be liked is if they do what everyone else is doing, and suddenly, everyone is doing something that they do not really want to do. Everyone gets caught up in doing whatever it was that no one actually wanted to do, and the end result is everyone being uncomfortable, complying only in hopes of being seen as though they were successfully being responsible.

. . .

*W*hen you make use of peer pressure, you will essentially be trying to make yourself do what you want the other person to do, or you will be bringing around other people that will also do what other people do. You may also attempt to convince the other person that, at the end of the day, other people that the target can relate to are all already doing what you are trying to get them to do. You would point out how people that your target can identify with would also be able to see how they were being impacted as well. You are essentially attempting to show the other person that, at the end of the day, they will also need to comply if they want to be in with the in crowd, so to speak.

*T*his is not actually that difficult to do. You would simply be bringing up the ways in which other people do what the target should be doing as well. You point out how you saw a bunch of people that you know that your target can relate to doing what you want them to do. You point out the ways in which you know that other people also do those particular things as well. Over time, as more and more of the pressure is laid on the individual, they begin to feel more and more convincing. Eventually, they feel like they have to comply. That feeling of being part of the group becomes too much to ignore and deny, and the end result is being stuck trying to make it work. When you feel like you have no choice but to comply, you are going to wind up struggling when you try to do anything else.

Repetition

Finally, the last method that will be mentioned for you here is the use of repetition to control the mind of someone else. When it comes right down to it, the mind is always listening. It is always

paying attention to the world around it. In particular, your unconscious mind is constantly aware of its surroundings from a wide
scale; it focuses on just about everything. It looks at the world
around you so you do not have to. Your unconscious mind is there,
constantly underneath the conscious, processing everything
around you while it is not in your conscious focus. You are still
able to react to what is around you because of this—but this comes
at a price. Your unconscious mind is constantly generalizing. It
takes in information and it takes in stimuli indiscriminately. This is
the concept that underlies the ability to use subliminal manipulation. You are essentially attempting to influence the unconscious
mind.

One way that you can influence the unconscious, then, is
through constant repetition. You can repeatedly reiterate
the point that you make. Slowly, but surely, that point gets internalized. Little by little, you begin to feel like there is real validity in
what is being said. You feel like, at the end of the day, you begin to
accept that idea at face value. You make it a point to listen to the
way in which you are being exposed to simply because you have
heard it enough time.

Think about it—how many lessons have you learned
simply from hearing your parents talk about them
repeatedly? How many concepts have you picked up on, how many
beliefs have you taken all because you have heard someone else
touting the point? Many people do not realize that this is a way
that they can be controlled, and that becomes readily apparent
when you consider the fact that advertisements work so well. You
may tune out the advertisements that you are exposed to, but at
the end of the day, you are still just as susceptible to them. In fact,

the next time that you are considering which brand of an item to buy, you will probably unconsciously reach for the brand that you have been exposed to more in your own attempts to shop for them. You will naturally gravitate toward them because your unconscious mind is biased. It has developed that bias over time thanks to the way in which you presented it to yourself. You have actually begun to pick up on those concepts just because of the constant exposure to advertisements.

Similarly, when you want to control someone else's mind, all you have to do is reiterate points subtly. You will bring up the same topic several times, in different contexts and in different settings, all trying to get someone to believe that you are better suited to doing what you want to do. When you want someone to believe what you are pushing, the best way to do so is through constant attempts to change the way in which the other person thinks. Essentially, you just find ways to fit that new subject into the discussion.

For example, if you think that people should get the best education possible, you would want to make sure that you tell them that education is best. Every time that it is time for you to talk to the other person, it makes sense for you to work to try to talk to them about what you are doing. It is important for you to pay attention to the ways in which you can subtly and quietly bring these points up without drawing attention. Of course, if you are constantly just walking around saying, "You should go and get an education!" to your partner, they will catch onto it. Thy will know that you are trying to push them into it and that does not usually work. Rather, you need to make them feel like the points that you bring up are their own thoughts so they do not feel like they need to try to take control. You do not want to make the other person feel like, at the end of the day, they are forced to listen to you. You do not want them to feel like they are listening to you; you want them to be able to come to that conclusion on their own. After all, the best way that you are able to remain undetected is if you are able to continually avoid getting blamed for the problem at hand. You need to be able to hind behind what you are doing.

The next time you want to try this, come up with something that you can say that is not going to draw much attention. You could even just have a single word or concept that you use. If you wanted Italian food for dinner, for example, you could have a conversation about the Mediterranean, pasta, Rome, and anything else that is tied to Italy or the idea of Italy, and then after the fact, ask what the other person wants to eat for dinner. If you can plant that idea in the back of their mind, they begin to feel like they want it. They begin to think in those ways that you want them to because their unconscious mind is picking up in everything. As this happens, little by little, you reach a point in which you are able to succeed in influencing the mind of the other person. You become skilled at being able to directly and carefully provide the other person with a way of thinking without them becoming aware of what you are doing.

USING NEURO-LINGUISTIC
PROGRAMMING

THIS NEXT CONCEPT that you are going to be introduced to is one known as neuro-linguistic programming. NLP is a common way in which people tap into the minds of other people. It is like a therapeutic form of mind control, existing to try to influence the way in which people behave. By using NLP, you are usually able to take control of wthe other person. You are able to influence the way that you think or feel so you can better see the way that the world works. You are effectively influencing the way that other people see and interact with the world when you use these methods. You are making it so that the other person that you are around is going to be influenced.

*O*nce again, with this particular form of control over someone else, you are looking at that same cycle between thoughts, feelings, and behaviors. You are looking at the fact that, at the end of the day, you are able to change the way that people act by changing their thoughts. However, this particular form of influence on other people also takes a close look at the ways in which you can control through the use of your own body.

*N*LP is somewhat unique in the sense that it creates a connection between you and the other person known as a rapport—this rapport is the way in which you are able to measure the bond between yourself and the other person. A good rapport is one in which you are held in a higher esteem. Essentially, when your rapport is better with someone else, you are trusted better. You are seen as a trustworthy individual that can be assumed to do the right thing, no matter what is going on. This opens up the other person's unconscious mind to you, much like you were seeking to do when you isolated and befriended the other person. When you are able to make sure that you and the other person have that bond with each other, you know that, at the end of the day, you have that sort of backdoor access to their actions. You can control them through the use of controlling yourself.

*N*LP was initially designed to be a way in which average people, with no psychology training, would be able to access their minds. It was designed to take the concepts of many different psychotherapies and apply them in a way that did not require years upon years to learn. These methods were designed to bring together the connection between thoughts and language and the behavioral trends that could be seen as a direct result of them.

*W*hen you make use of these processes, you get that access to the mind. You get that ability to be able to better deal with people. You learn how you can better control other people in ways that will allow you to better take command of what is going on around them. You are able to change their behaviors by getting them to follow your own lead without realizing it.

*W*ithin this chapter, we are going to delve into the world of NLP. We are going to look at the ways in which you can make better use of these processes. We are going to understand what the principles behind NLP are. We will look at the way that you can trigger mirroring to create that rapport that you will need to start the use of NLP. Then, we will take a look at several of the other methods that you can use to ensure that, at the end of the day, you can control people. Remember, you are able to influence the minds of other people with ease if you are able to put these principles to good use. If you can ensure that you do learn to use the principles, encouraging them and making sure that they happen, you will know that you can influence the way that people behave. You will know that you can influence the way that they think and feel. You will be able to convince them to do things that they did not realize that they would be willing to do.

What is Neuro-Linguistic Programming?

NLP is a method in which you are able to communicate with the other person in order to influence what they are doing. Essentially, you are attempting to communicate your own desires to the other person without overwhelming them. It is indirect—it is making an attempt to alter their own thoughts by interacting with just their unconscious mind.

*W*ithin NLP, you will see the idea that the mind is separated out. The mind has two key components: The conscious and the unconscious and they do not regularly communicate with each other. On the contrary, they exist almost on two completely different spectrums. They communicate entirely differently—think of it as if your conscious mind speaks one language while your unconscious mind speaks another. No matter how hard you try to get them to come together, you cannot get that sort of cohesion that you need. However, with NLP, you get to bridge that gap. With NLP, you can effectively allow yourself to better control people through the use of being able to look at how you can engage with the unconscious mind to get the conscious results that you want.

*T*he unconscious mind underlies everything, but for good reason—it is able to control everything that you do and alter the way in which you think of everything around you. It allows you to better control the world around you. It allows you to better cope with the ways in which you can deal with the world around you. It watches to protect you from the world around you. It learns patterns so you do not have to worry about them. It will effectively allow you to control the way that you see the world.

*W*hen you take control of the other person's unconscious mind, you are able to slowly and subtly change it. You slowly and carefully work to try to change their mind. You do this through many different means. Some people, for example, will make use of the way that they speak. They can control the minds of those around them through ensuring that they use vocabulary that they know will allow them to get that control that they want. They us words that will plant ideas in the unconscious mind, much like we discussed already. When you do this, you can better use the fact that your words are powerful.

· · ·

*Y*ou can also use your body to communicate with other people, altering the way that they perceive the world by using your own body language or movements. You can teach people to be conditioned to your gestures, much like how you can teach a dog to obey the way that you move your hand. When you teach someone else to interact like this, you can essentially take control of them with movements.

*E*ffectively, you can use any of the senses to take control of the individuals. You can change the way that you speak. You can create associations between the individual and what they listen to. You can change the way in which you are able to talk to people to try to get them to better become influenced by you. The best part of it all is that they learn this all without them ever having to know that they are.

*T*he idea with NLP is that everyone has this one distinct way in which they see the world. It is their own perception of the world around them—their map of reality. However, those maps of reality are constantly being changed. They are not what is in front of the individual, but rather, the way that people see the world around them. With the way that you interact with other people, you can alter the way that they see the world. You can change those maps of reality so you can better influence the way that you are trying to

*W*hen you make use of NLP, then, you are actively interacting with that map of reality. You are actively reaching into their minds and changing the ways that they choose to behave. The more that you do this, the better you become at being able to control others. At the root of this, the idea is that if you can present the other person with an act, a thought, or a behavior, you must first encourage it on your own.

Mirroring

Before we get into the methods that you can use NLP to control other people, you must first look at the ways in which you can understand them and get them to trust you enough. Rapport, that judgment of how good or bad your relationship with someone else is, is that metric that you will use. Rapport is not something that you can put a number to, nor is it something that you can ask about. However, you can see it when you look at other people and the way that they behave. When you stop and study other people, you can, however, begin to see that rapport played out. Rapport is seeing in the ways that people mirror each other.

Think about it—you can tell how close people are to each other based on the ways that they move. You can tell how close someone is to someone else, not just by the physical proximity, but also by watching whether or not they are mirroring the other person. Mirroring is the act of mimicking. It is that idea that you and someone else are on the same page. It is looking at whether what you are doing is being reflected by the other person as well. When you mirror someone else, you are essentially mimicking their behaviors.

People that are on the same page as each other, people who trust each other, and people who like each other all tend to do the same thing: They mirror. They copy back the behaviors that they see in other people. This is thanks to mirror neurons—the neurons that you have in your body that are designed to provide empathy. They are the areas within your own brain that activate when you see someone else doing what you are doing. When you see someone else that is doing something, the same areas of your brain activate—but only in the mirror neurons. This is also the reason that people empathize with other people as well.

*N*LP tries to take advantage of this idea. It looks at the ways that you will be able to latch onto those behaviors and really take advantage of them. NLP practitioners encourage this—they will essentially tell you or show you that you must be able to change the way that you behave by changing their own behaviors. When you want to make use of NLP, you must first make sure that the connection that you need is created. You need to get the other person to mirror you. It is not until they are mirroring you that you will be able to truly activate your ability to control them.

*N*ow, you could wait for this to develop naturally over time. You could see that over time, you do gradually form that relationship with the person that you are looking to control. However, more realistically, you will probably want to cut to the chase. You will not want to waste all of that time trying to build up that rapport naturally when you are trying to control someone else quickly. For that situation, you are in luck—you can make use of the process of mirroring.

· · ·

*M*irroring as a technique is when you trigger the action yourself. You do this by makings sure that you start mirroring the other person rather than waiting for them to mirror you. Their mind will catch on to the fact that you are mirroring them and as a direct result, they will begin to mimic you back. Their mind will automatically deem that you must not be a threat or rather, that you must be someone that is trustworthy, thanks to the way that you are behaving. If they see that you are regularly following their lead, they will naturally reciprocate it— they will begin to mirror you back. You create that sort of flattery that they need and you then unlock their mind in the process.

*W*hen you wish to mirror someone else, there are four steps that you have to take. If you can take these four steps, you should find that everything else falls into place naturally and easily.

1. Start by giving the other person your utter attention. You should be able to watch the other person and think that they are the most interesting person to you at this point in time. You want to ensure that you see them as being deserving of your attention at that one point in time. You will focus on theme entirely at this point in time. Give them your utter focus. Face them squarely—this means that you must align your body to them. Give them your eye contact. Really listen to them.

2. Then, as you begin to feel connected to this other person, it is time for you to shift gears. You need to begin to mimic them at this point. You can choose to start copying their body language, but usually speaking, that becomes too apparent too quickly. They catch onto what you are doing

and that destroys the effectiveness of it. When the mind realizes that you are actively attempting to copy it, they begin to feel like you are being weird. Think of how annoying it can be when a child runs around mimicking you—it would bother you if an adult did the same. However, the unconscious mind is flattered by it. You need to find some sort of intermediary that allows for this process to happen without you feeling like you cannot control it. For this reason, it can be easier to try to hide your intentions by mimicking something that is not as readily apparent. For example, you can make use of mirroring other parts of their body language. Perhaps one of the easiest to do is the voice. You can mimic their tone and their pace. You match them at this point. Try to make it so your own voice follows along with theirs. You should be speaking with the same intensity that they feel. You should be attempting to match their same intonation and speech patterns. You must do this all without being noticed, however—do not make obvious changes; simply naturally follow their lead and allow their own vocal patterns to lead the way.

3. With the pacing done, you must now really seal the deal. The best way to seal that deal is through the use of what is known as a punctuator. A person's punctuator is a way that they are able to emphasize something. It is being able to stop and move in a certain way that shows precisely what is being talked about. It tells you when to pay attention to what the individual is thinking or what they are saying. It is essentially the exclamation point of the vocal or the body language. It is necessary to be able to activate this to trigger mirroring. Essentially, you will want to watch the other person until they prepare to make use of their own punctuator again. Then, right when you can see that they

are about to use their own punctuator, you beat them to the punch. Make use of it there. It could be that they use a raise of their brows or they may emphasize what they are saying with a hand motion or anything else. No matter the way that they use it, you must meet it. It is only then that you really begin to trigger that sudden relationship of mirroring. They feel totally understood at this point. They know that you know what they mean and that brings them to wanting to mirror you in return.

4. Finally, the last step is the testing step. This is where you are able to essentially discover if what you have done has worked or if you will need to try again. What you will need to do is take a moment to move your own body subtly. Make sure that you move it in a way that is not going to be too obvious, but is also not going to be something that would be a mere coincidence. You want to see if they also mirror you when you do this. Start with something small—it could be brushing your hair out of your face or adjusting your sleeve or just about anything. If you have done the job right, you have triggered that mirroring relationship and they are now mirroring you, too. This means that you would have managed to better convince them that they do need to mirror you. If they mimic your own movements, you have succeeded. If not, go back to step 2 and continue down the process for a while longer. You will trigger them to follow along eventually—it is just a matter of when it happens.

Weasel Words

Another common method to manipulate people is through the sheer use of language. You are going to change the way that you word what you are doing to try to get the other person's mind to follow your own lead. You do this in many different ways; you can, for example, encourage someone else to buy something by the way that you phrase the question. All you have to do is alter the way that you present what you are saying. For example, imagine that you sell appliances. It is a hefty purchase and you get a lot of people that come in, look around, window shop for a while, but do not actually buy, specifically because they are looking at expensive appliances and they need to determine whether or not they should spend that much money on something or whether they are better of continuing to shop elsewhere.

When you want to get them to buy, then, you ask questions in a way that naturally leads them exactly where you want them. Instead of asking, "Would you like to buy?" you can ask them questions that make it more finalized. You approach the situation and use language like it is already decided, such as saying, "When you buy this..." instead of, "If you buy this..." When you shift the focus to when instead of if, you essentially encourage them to start thinking as if they are going to buy it. The unconscious mind is listening and the unconscious mind then latches onto that idea. The unconscious mind then begins to behave as if it is already decided. This happens regularly and usually influences people into seeing when they should buy.

Other examples of weasel words include saying, "If you were to..." in order to imply that there is an option there, but the unconscious mind will immediately latch onto it. You may also use phrases such as:

- After you...
- As you...

- You may realize...
- You may experience...
- When you notice...

As you can see, they are all vague, ambiguous phrases that can have a lot of impact on how the individual is thinking at that point of time. When you use these on the regular, you get to plant thoughts without them being noticed. All you have to do is remember the proper structure. You must make sure that you combine a command phrase with a state that you want to imply, plus the tonality that shows that you are commanding it. When you can make sure that all three of these criteria are met, you will realize that you can, in fact, lead other people's minds as well.

*L*et's look back for a moment at the phrase of "When you buy this, you will notice that it is better than the others." You have your commanding phrase—"When you buy this." You have your condition that you are implying: "You will notice." Then, all that is left for you to do is make sure that when you provide it, you speak with a commanding tone. When you can commit to that, you can usually alter the way that those around you speak.

Anchoring

Anchoring is one of the most quintessentially NLP methods that you can use. It I a way in which you can condition someone else to associate two states together. It is often used to try to trigger positive feelings on command for people that are typically in need of that assistance. However, you can use it to anchor other actions as well. Some people like to anchor feelings of pleasure around them to the movement of a hand. Some people like to use these methods to make their friends or family more confident. You may be able to end an argument by conditioning a partner to apologize and stop arguing to the motion of a hand. You can use this method in so many different situations, and all you have to do is start the conditioning so you can draw from it.

*E*ssentially, all you have to do here is figure out a way in which you can condition the other person. You are trying to pair a specific state that you want them to be in with an action that you perform. Think back to the way that dogs can be conditioned to salivate to the sound of a bell being rung. Just as Pavlov was able to condition his dogs, you can condition just about anyone else as well. All you have to do is identify a few key points.

*F*irstly, you must make sure that you know what it is that you would like to condition. What is the feeling or the response that you want to be able to trigger on a whim? You also need to have the stimulus—this is the anchor that you will use that will be the trigger. Finally, you will need to make use of the necessary techniques that you will need to trigger the condition that you are looking for.

*L*et's say that you want to condition your partner to feel like he or she must apologize when you move your hand in a very specific manner. You then would need to decide how you will trigger that apology in the first place. There are many different ways that this could happen—you could convince them to trigger those responses through the use of causing some sort of accident that they then naturally apologize for. For example, you could move a bit closer so they bump into you and then they say that they are sorry out of politeness.

84

. . .

*W*hen you have everything identified, all you need to do is repeat the processes over and over. Make your partner apologize, then use your trigger that you want them to associate with the apology. Then, you simply reinforce it over time. You must repeat this process for a while. The more that you do, the more likely it is that you will be able to get them to continue to be triggered into apologies in this manner.

*A*fter enough reiteration, you will find that your partner does give in. You can test this relatively easily. The next time you are being talked to, for example, you could try using your anchor. If your partner trails off and apologized for something, such as bothering you or something else, you know that you have succeeded. If not, however, you know that you will need to continue to try to create that connection. It will not be effective or you until you notice that they are regularly apologizing back to you whenever you use the trigger.

Pace and Lead

Finally, the last method that we will discuss for NLP is the pace and lead method. This is a method in which you are able to regularly and readily change the body language of someone else that relies heavily on mirroring. To begin using this, you must be able to first trigger that state of mirroring. When it is there, you must then match the other person's pace. You are doing this because you are attempting to alter what they are doing. For example, perhaps they are tapping their hand against the table while you are talking and it is really bothering you. You do not want to say anything in the moment. However, you can begin to slow their behaviors down as well. You start by pacing. To pace is to match their current pace.

You follow what they are doing for the moment before you start to lead them as well. In this instance, for example, you may cross your arms, but drum your fingers against one of them, to the same rhythm that the other person is.

To lead the other person, you can start slowly altering the way that you are behaving. You slowly begin to change the pace of what they are doing. Perhaps you slow down the tapping on your arm. You slow it little by little, watching as they continue to shift their own pace to match yours as well. Then, when their pace slows enough, you can slowly stop, and watch how they do as well.

This can be used in other ways too. You can use it to lead the behaviors of someone else. You can use it to get people to change the direction that they are walking. You can use it to take control of a situation. When you use this, you are essentially placing yourself in the place of the leader without the other person realizing what you are doing.

USING THE POWER OF PERSUASION

UNDERLYING many convincing methods to use for control or manipulation of other people are a series of principles for people. These principles are known as the principles of persuasion—they allow you to better control the way in which other people think— but these do not require the same degree of secrecy that many other methods throughout this book use. They are overt with their suggestions. When you are attempting to persuade someone else, they know exactly what it is that you want. They know precisely what it is because you ask them for it directly. However, you must also recognize that, at the end of the day, you cannot be successful with these methods if you were to tell someone that you were using them. It is not what you are saying here that is manipulative or that has the power- it is the way that the mind responds that is relevant.

*A*t the end of the day, persuasion is incredibly powerful. It consists of the ability to word things in just the right way, to phrase your argument in the most convincing manner that you can, that allows you to get other people to better agree with you. Persuasion is powerful. Persuasion allows you to better interact with the world around you. Persuasion teaches you that you can use your words to control the situation.

*W*ithin this chapter, we are going to address the methods of persuading people. We are going to look at what persuasion itself is. This is a very important concept to understand—it can work out in nearly any context to some degree. You must be able to become persuasive if you want to be influential or successful—the most successful people out there are those that know how to persuade people. They are the ones that know how they can word what they want in just the right way that other people will willingly play along. They will gladly do what they are asked because they know that they have chosen to do so and they like the reasons that they were asked to do so. They will choose to make these decisions, provided with the information that they need to feel compelled to do so.

*I*f you are in sales as a career line, this is a skillset that you need. It is manipulative in the sense that you can make great use of these principles. It is manipulative in the sense that if you do use these, you are able to essentially control the mind of someone else. However, they are also not manipulative in many other contexts as well. It is important for you to recognize that the methods that are provided here are also very valid tools that you can regularly use. They are valid tools that can be used to try to convince other people to do what you wish. It is valid to persuade people to do something and it is not always inherently harmful.

· · ·

 *U*ltimately, you can look at persuasion in two ways: It can be seen within the context of the principles of persuasion, which are six principles that are incredibly powerful. These principles define the way in which the mind works. They identify the ways that people are oftentimes convinced to do what they do and how you can take advantage of the mind's tendencies to convince other people of what you want them to do. You can also consider persuasion within the context of rhetoric. Rhetoric is the formal articulation of the way of being persuasive that dates back to the philosopher Aristotle.

Principles of Persuasion

The six principles of persuasion are the ways in which you can directly alter the mind of someone else. They tell you how you can be the most compelling that you can be. When you are able to use these principles to your own devices, you are able to get people to do whatever it is that you wish of them. You can usually get them to better agree with them all by tapping into these six principles that directly relate back to the brain. Each of these work on different subconscious levels—they work because the individual is not aware of the way that you are altering your own patterns. They do not see that what you are doing is there to deliberately alter the way that they are behaving. They do not realize that you are intentionally attempting to get them to change their own minds or that you are intentionally taking control of them. They do not realize that, at the end of the day, you are controlling this all thanks to the way that you choose to present yourself. While you are being entirely transparent with the other person about what you want them to do and you are giving them the information that you know that they need to make a decision, you are also taking the steps that you will need to allow yourself to better influence them.

• • •

Reciprocity

The first principle that we are taking a look at is reciprocity. This is the idea that when you do something for someone else, they naturally want to return the favor. It does not need to be anything grand at all- rather, you simply need to do something for the other person that makes them feel more compelled to do something in return for you as well. Imagine that you are a car salesperson. When you are meeting with a prospective client that has children, you may offer to give the children a lollipop or a snack to try to keep them calm and the parents see this extension of your kindness and they will naturally, unconsciously, also want to be able to do something in return for you as well. Does this mean that they will buy a car simply because you have given their children a lollipop? Not at all—but you do make yourself seem that much more deserving of their consideration. They are more likely to want to give back to you thanks to the fact that you have given to them and their family.

This is a very common principle that people use regularly. You can see it when people send out deals to try to entice you to sign up. They tell you to sign up and get a gift today in hopes that you will want to continue to stay onboard later as well. Being able to reciprocate is a very powerful tool. It works because at the end of the day, reciprocity is a very important survival aspect for social species such as people. We are social by nature and the best way to survive as a social species is for some degree of reciprocity to be considered. When you use reciprocity in a natural setting, you are looking out for someone else's needs most of the time. By looking out for someone else's needs, when you need help, you know that the person that you helped is going to likely volunteer where they can, simply because you have helped them. This keeps the whole species alive, even if you get caught up in something. When you are able to fall back on this, you know that you are better able to keep everyone alive. You know that the species as a whole is much more likely to thrive and that means that you are much more likely to be able to continue on as a species.

*B*ecause reciprocity is something that is evolutionarily advantageous when everyone is also reciprocal, you know that you are more likely than not to find someone that will behave in this manner, meaning that you can often take advantage of it.

*C*onsistency and commitment

*A*t the end of the day, we all are looking for consistency. Consistency is familiar and comfortable. It is something that we can rely on while knowing that at the end of the day, we will be able to predict what will happen next. Because we naturally value people that are committed and consistent, we also tend to naturally fall into those habits. We have a tendency to shift into that consistency to allow ourselves to be seen as reliable and dependable. However, this brings with it other complications as well. When you fall into these habits and tendencies, you become predictable.

. . .

*T*his principle draws upon that fact. Statistically speaking, once you get someone to commit to something, no matter how small or insignificant it is, you can usually get them to continue to agree later on as well. Because you can regularly get people to commit in these manners, you know that you are better able to take advantage of a situation if you can get a small commitment first. This particular principle reaches out for that smaller commitment. It looks for that little shift in behaviors that will also allow for the development of what is going on.

*T*o use this principle, all you have to do is get someone to agree to something prior to you attempting to get them to do what you really want. If you want to make use of this to, for example, convince someone to stay at work late for you so you can go home early, you would probably start by firstly getting a smaller commitment. You may, for example, ask if they can do something for you really quickly at work. If you ask them to do that for you, such as asking them to run something to the other room or to grab something from the printer, you already have them in an agreeable mood and that means that you can continue to take advantage of the situation at hand. After they have agreed to do something for you, you can then shift to asking them to do something that is more demanding or more high-stakes. After they have agreed to help you with something small, you have already shifted them into that state of cooperation that you will need to pull from. When you can get that done, you can then get through the rest of it with ease.

Social proof

. . .

*W*e are right back to a fundamental principle that has been mentioned repeatedly throughout this book—the desire to be consistent with everyone else. Social proof is essentially getting the other person that you are trying to convince to do something to give in for social reasons. You are laying on the peer pressure to do this—you are essentially working to make them feel like the entire group is doing something. This is why when something does get busy, more and more people all naturally gravitate toward it. You may see that some people naturally tend to gravitate toward what is "in" at the moment. Look at a high school or a shopping mall and you will see this—everyone usually wears the same style, no matter whether they really like it or not. When something is trendy, everyone follows it. Everyone feels like they have to keep up with the group. People will choose the crowded restaurant over the one that is not crowded because they assume that the popular one is probably better. Humans have a tendency to allow for their minds to be made for them on the regular. They oftentimes tend to just default because it is easier to default to what everyone else is doing than it is to take a risk and potentially not fit in.

*B*ecause people will always want to be liked and they will always want to fit in with the group because humans are a social species, you will always see this principle work. Unless you are dealing with one of the people out there that intentionally flouts over social expectations or norms, you can usually be pretty sure that this principle will be effective.

. . .

*I*f you are trying to get someone to sign a petition, then, you may weigh heavily on how everyone else in the neighborhood agreed, or bring up the names of big people that also agree with the principle of the petition. You may try to say that other people within someone's demographic are already commonly buying something to try to sell it to more. You can see that commercials use this as well—commercials for diapers often show brand new mothers cuddling their newborn infants and then talk about how mothers and hospitals both agree about something.

*T*o use this yourself, then, all you have to do is identify the crowd that your target belongs to and then appeal to that. Point out how other people in that position also do what you are trying to get them to do. When you do that regularly, you are usually able to get the person to agree.

*A*uthority

*A*uthority is perhaps one of the easiest principles that you can appeal to. All you have to do is make yourself an expert or an authority in some way, shape, or form. If you can establish why it is that you should be listened to, you can usually also get them to agree that you should be listened to. Think about it this way—if you are going to go to the doctor to get looked at, are you going to take medical advice from the receptionist, the nurse, or the doctor more? Most people will always weigh the advice of the doctor higher than the other two people, regardless of whether they are right or not. This is simply because they will naturally tend to assume that the doctor is the one that has the most experience. This is true for the most part—usually, doctors do have that expertise.

To further reiterate this point, if you or your partner were pregnant, would you listen to the advice of an obstetrician or a podiatrist when it came down to what the pregnant woman should do? Most people would naturally side with the OB —they do not see why they would not listen to the one that has the expertise in the particular condition and field. People will always gravitate toward the one that has the most experience, no matter what it is.

To use this principle, then, all you have to do is establish in some way that you are the expert. You can do this in many different ways. You could, for example, put up your diploma in your office that touts the major that you got a degree in. You could choose to put up pictures of your clients, happy and enjoying whatever it is that you did for them. You could have a sign up in your lobby that advertises how many people that you have helped. Essentially, you want to make use of this principle by making it clear that you do have the experience that you need to justify being the one that is listened to. If you can make that happen, you are usually going to find that you can properly get those around you to listen as well.

 iking

. . .

This one may seem a bit strange, but at the same time, it makes perfect sense—the more likable that you are, the more likely you are to be seen as credible and convincing. If you try to convince someone that likes you, they are far more likely to agree with you than someone that does not like you. This is due to the fact that we have these subtle tendencies that will play a part here. You must be able to recognize that, at the end of the day, the more likable you are, the more likely it is that people are going to want to help you. People will naturally gravitate toward doing what you need if you are likeable and this is for a very specific reason. We naturally identify with those that we like. When we like someone, we believe that we have something in common. It may be that they have a similarity to you and you feel like you can better relate. That is a fair point—but it is also a point that can be very easily and readily exploited without much effort.

To make use of this principle, all you have to do, then, is make sure that you make yourself likable. You must interact with someone, if they are a stranger, in a way that you become relatable. This is why so often, in meetings or negotiations, there will be some sort of icebreaker done to loosen up the crowd. When that icebreaker happens, you can then begin to relate better to those around you and that means that you can better interact.

To make yourself likable, then, you can try checking three points in your interaction with the other person. You can:

- Make yourself seem more human—try having pictures of

yourself and your family up in the office or relate back to the other person. If you see that they are wearing a football shirt, relate to it somehow, for example. If they have young children and you do, too, share that with them. You can make use of this principle to help yourself better relate to the other person and therefore make yourself seem more likable.

- Make them feel good about themselves—people naturally like the people that make them feel good and you can oftentimes do that with these of a compliment or some other method of trying to relate to them. You could say that you like their hair or that they are choosing a car that you like or anything else that will make them feel validated and therefore, better. The tirck, however, is that you must make sure that you really mean what you say. You needto be genuine or they will see right through your attempt to make them feel better, defeating the entire purpose of what you are doing.

- Make yourself cooperative—make sure that you tell them that you are working together. By making sure that you are both part of a cooperative team with a cooperative goal, you are better able to remind them that you are in it with them. You can remind them that you are on their side and in doing so they will begin to like you more. This is where the popularity of the phrase, "Help me help you," came from.

Scarcity

*F*inally, the last principle to consider is the principle of scarcity. When you are looking at something being scarce, its value will always go up. People naturally want to gravitate toward things that are not as readily available. If something is deemed to be scarce and therefore valuable, people will flock for it. You see this often—people regularly make use of, for example, trying to get the newest limited supply or limited edition items. It is not because they genuinely want it—they simply want it because it is in demand. Think about how many different fast food restaurants and cafes tend to make use of this. They will regularly circulate in seasonal items, sometimes so well that the item itself becomes a sort of trendy phenomenon of its own, such as the way that pumpkin spice became the flavor that defines the market from early August until Thanksgiving. This high demand of the flavor is driven up by the fact that you can only really find it readily available during this season, and the market for it has spread dramatically. What was once a coffee flavor can now be found as a cookie, as a candle, a perfume, cereal, oatmeal, and just about any other baked good or treat. It became incredibly valuable thanks to the fact that it was limited and everyone wants it. There are always lines for that first pumpkin spice latte at the beginning of the season. Likewise, when something else is scarce, such as a limited edition item, it will always be desired by people. The value of it goes up immensely, not because it is genuinely popular, but because it is scarce.

To make use of this yourself, then, your job is to figure out some way that you can better make other people see what you are doing or the deals that you are offering as scarce. You can do this in relationships as well—you see this with the ultimatum of "Do this or I'm breaking up with you." When you put this ultimatum into place, you make yourself scarce. Suddenly, you are in demand because of the very real threat of not being there in the first place. The idea of not being able to get something in the future means that it becomes more in demand. People naturally want it more because it is not as guaranteed.

Rhetoric

The other way that we are going to talk about persuasion is through the use of rhetoric. Rhetoric is a form of speech that is meant to be effective in persuading other people. It was defined to make itself become persuasive and compelling to motivate people to change their views or actions. It is making sure that you word things in just the right manner to ensure that, at the end of the day, you can ensure that everyone is convinced of what you have to say.

*R*hetoric involves the use of three basic principles: The appeal to authority or character, the appeal to emotion, and the appeal to logic. Each of these work slightly differently, but the end result is that you should be able ot become more persuasive by making sure that these elements get included in what you are doing.

*A*ppeal to authority or character

*W*hen you want to appeal to the character or authority of someone else, you must make them become someone that is inherently worth listening to in some way. You must ensure that the way that you have presented what you are presenting is compelling and therefore something that you should be following. You must ensure that you are putting together a compelling reason that you should be listened to. You may use an appeal to authority for this, and some people certainly do. However, you may also use other methods as well, such as talking about what it is that makes you worthy of being listened to. For example, what is it about your personality that made you so successful at running your business? What trials did you go through to get to the point that you are at now When you look at these different character traits, they should become something tha tis compelling and worthy of consideration so you are better able to convince other people to commit to what you are pushing for. If you can get them to commit, you are much more likely to persuade them.

his is oftentimes done with compelling backstories or experiences explained during meetings. They are ways that you are able to point out that you do know what you are doing and that you do know how to do what you are doing. They are designed to allow yourself to better deal with the ways that you should interact and in doing so, they are designed to convince other people to deem you to be compelling enough to follow.

ppeal to emotion

n appeal to emotion is set to cause some sort of emotion that will be compelling into the target or into the audience. To use this method, you attempt to add information to the story that you are weaving to the person that you are trying to convince that will trigger those feelings. You can do this in pointing out the unfortunate events that happened to someone that did not follow your advice, for example. You could make use of trying to get someone into a good mood to get them to want to agree with you. You could try to make them feel more interested in donating to a cause by showing images of the people that will be helped.

*N*o matter what the method that you use for this, one thing is true: The negative emotions tend to be the most powerful. If you want someone to be compelled to act in a way that will incite change, you must find a way to convince them with the negative emotions. You can trigger people to act because they want to free themselves from that negativity. They want to remain in a state of positivity and that means that they do not want to be held back by these bad feelings.

*A*ppeal to logic

*F*inally, the appeal to logic is the way in which you are able to persuade people to act through the use of numbers. You are trying to come up with an argument that is so compelling, the individual cannot reject it. Oftentimes, however, these methods do not even have to be logically sound in the first place. You can use the use of throwing statistics and numbers at someone else in hopes of them feeling like they must agree with you simply because you must be right when that is not necessarily the case. You are trying to convince them that they must do this and they choose to do so because they do not want to try to figure out how to follow the math that you provide.

· · ·

*T*his is usually used with an overwhelming use of numbers and math. If you can fall back on this, you may find that those around you that fall for it are actually convinced not because you are right, but because you *sound* right. Try adding in statistics that may be somewhat relevant to your arguments to try to make it more compelling to those around you. People will naturally agree with the ways that people attempt to convince them to change what they are doing when they feel like the facts say that they must.

USING BODY LANGUAGE TO MANIPULATE

FINALLY, the last method of manipulation that we are going to consider within this book is the use of body language. Body language is incredibly powerful. It is incredibly compelling. It can be used in many different manners that allow for you to directly control and influence other people. Thanks to the fact that body language is nonverbal and the unconscious mind tends to rule over it, people often do not notice when you are using body language to try to influence them. They do not see that you are influencing them simply because they do not consciously watch the way that you move. They simply get these sort of gut reactions that tell them how they should be responding to what is around them. They feel compelled to act but they do not really think about why they feel that compulsion in the first place—they simply make it happen.

hen you are attempting to use body language to control other people, you are simply tapping into

that unconscious tendency. You are allowing yourself to influence other people because you know how they work. You understand that the unconscious mind is always watching and always engaging. You know that the unconscious mind is responsible for the feelings that they have. You take advantage of this—and unless the other person happens to be pretty in touch with their own body language and has gotten good at paying attention to the ways in which they must change their own, you are likely to see that you can alter what they are doing.

The Power of Body Language

Body language is incredibly powerful. When you make use of body language, you are looking at controlling the vast majority of the communication that happens between people. What many people do not realize is that for the most part, communication is nonverbal. We spend most of our communication trying to engage with people nonverbally. You can see this clearly when you are looking at how people respond to you. The way that you approach someone else is incredibly telling—when you run ant someone with a scowl, you are naturally going to see them react first in fear and then possibly in anger if they decide to fight back. Your body language and the way that you hold and present yourself can greatly change the way in which the other person that you are interacting with sees you. You can take advantage of this regularly —you can ensure that you are better able to control the others. You can see that you are much more likely to be able to control them just by making sure that you present yourself the right way.

$\mathcal{T}$he way that you move will naturally trigger the other person's unconscious mind. Their unconscious mind will register what you are doing and create feelings. Those feelings will then directly influence the way that the other person interacts with you. You can make someone feel like a child with the way that you look at them, or you can make them feel at ease. You can scare someone, dominate someone, or even attract someone, all by the way that you present yourself. Learning to control your body language may be difficult at first, but if you can master it, you can constantly be controlling the ways that you influence those around you. You can determine how you present yourself so you can then ensure that the other person reacts the way that you want them to. It is not always guaranteed, but you can usually create these reactions.

Body Language to Lead

The body language of leaders is typically that of confidence. If you want to lead a group or be considered a competent leader, the best way to make this happen is to ensure that you are able to better be deemed as a confident person. Confidence and leadership go hand in hand and people will almost always engage more with the people that they deem to be as more confident just due to the fact that confidence is typically seen as being something that that is trustworthy. When you want to make sure that you change your body language to that of a leader, then, you want to try to make use of the following changes:

- **Eye contact:** To engage with people with decent eye contact will help you to be seen as confident. However, the catch here is that your eye contact with the other person should not be seen as dominant or overbearing. You are not trying to intimidate someone here—you are trying to find a way that you can better relate to them. You are trying ot show that you are listening and therefore that you are paying attention, but also that you are not afraid to make that eye contact in the first place. When you make use of this, you can usually ensure that the other person does not worry about what you are trying to present to them.

- **Standing tall:** To be confident is to keep your own body language tall. You are looking to stand in a way that will be seen as confident. When you are tall and confident, you must keep your head level. Straighten out your spine, but do not tilt your head back to look down your nose. Rather, you should always be looking straight at people.
- **Release tension:** Tension screams nervousness and if you want to be assertively calm, you will want to make sure that you can release that tension just enough that you will be able to control what you are doing. You want to be able to show that, at the end of the day, you are not nervous, but rather, you are in complete and utter control.
- **Open body language:** You should keep your body language open to be deemed as confident. This means no crossed arms and no crossing your legs, either. Do not hide behind any items and be able to remove any barriers between yourself and those around you.
- **Talk with your hands:** When you talk with your hands, you keep them busy, but you also prevent yourself from falling into the trap of being too nervous or fidgeting with your hands. When your hands are unnaturally still or you try to hide them in your pockets or somewhere else, you tell the other person that you are hiding something.

Body Language to Dominate

Dominant body language is another type of body language to consider as well. You can use this to essentially intimidate those around you. You use it to try to show the other person that you are in control and at the top of the pecking order. Dominant body language is particularly useful to use if you are trying to prove that, at the end of the day, you are in control of everything going on. It is your way of showing that you get to be the one in control rather than anyone else. To dominate people, whether at home or in the workplace, or anywhere else, there are some very simple body language rules that you should follow to ensure that, at the end of the day, you are the one that gets to control what is going on. A lot of dominant body language is about going as open as possible. When you are dominating space, you are taking it all up. You are essentially asserting that you are the one in control. You tell everyone around you that you matter more than others and that you will get what you want, how you want it.

- **Widen your stance:** The wider your stances are, the more confident you become, and generally, anything beyond shoulder-width is immediately deemed to be dominant. Dominant behavior is essentially a step past confident behavior; it is your way of showing that you are the one that is in complete and utter control of a situation and that you are the one that gets to make all of the decisions. Stand as widely as you can and as tall as you can. You want to make sure that you are as big as you can make yourself so you know that you are able to control what is going on around you.
- **Hands on hips:** When you shift your hands so they are on your hips, you naturally expand your arms. You do this to be able to control the way that you are seen by the other person. You become larger than before, much like a cobra extending its hood or animals attempting to puff up. This makes you seem bigger and therefore more dominant and in control.
- **Head up, chin high:** When you hold your head up with

your chin out and high, you are essentially making it clear that you are in control. You are widening your stance so you are able to appear taller. This also allows you to be able to look down your nose, which is immediately going to make you appear larger than the other person. This trick works even if you are shorter than the other person; the appearance of looking down your nose is enough.

- **Position yourself higher:** Another common method that is used to dominate is to make sure that you are immediately higher up than everyone else around you. You can do this by using a chair with a higher setting than those that you will be working with, for example, or positioning yourself at the highest seat at the table or otherwise making sure that you are at the top physically. If everyone has to look up to you, you are automatically deemed more dominant whether they realize it or not.

- **Spread out:** When you are able to, you should also attempt to claim as much space around you as possible. Take up a bit more space at the table than is comfortably yours. Allow yourself to essentially encroach on what everyone else is doing. Take up their space without being willing to make concessions. You are essentially showing that you are more dominant because you have more space at the table or in the area.

- **Touch other people or their belongings:** When you want to declare dominance over someone else, the best way to do so is through touch. Touch the other person, typically on the arm or holding onto their handshake after you notice that they have already loosened their grip. Your lingering touch after they have pulled back shows that you are in control. Similarly, when you pat them on the shoulder or on the back when they go past you, you show that you are the one in control of that particular situation. When you touch their belongings, you also essentially claim it—you are taking over their personal space and their items, showing that you are not afraid to violate those norms or their own personal bubble.

- **Walk in the center of the space without moving:** When two people approach each other on a sidewalk or while walking down the street, they oftentimes will move over to make space for the other person. It is simply common courtesy to make space for the other person and it says that you respect them. However, when you are claiming dominance, you are not willing to give that space to them. You claim it all to yourself and refuse to share it.

- **Stare:** The stare, especially when unwavering and intense, is one of the greatest ways that you can declare dominance over a group. When you stare at other people, you usually make them uncomfortable—and for good reason. It is typically considered aggressive to stare endlessly and it makes people nervous. If you want to show that you are dominant, try staring with a neutral, or slightly displeased expressions. You will essentially create your own state of dominance over the other person.

Body Language to Attract

Finally, if you want to attract another person, there are ways that you can do so with a simple look. You can use your own body language to subtly plant the idea that you are interested in some sort of relationship, whether physical or romantic, with the other person and if you can make good use of how you present this, you can usually ensure that they are more likely to reciprocate. When you want to attract someone else, you may be worried about coming off too strongly, but ultimately, no matter what it is that you want out of a relationship, there are some telltale ways to pass that message along that are likely to be picked up and well-received. The body language in this section, unless noted, is typically gender-neutral.

- **The look-over:** This is that behavior where you see someone look at your eyes, then all the way down and back up your body. Especially when paired with a positive expressions, this is a good sign that someone likes what they see. When you do this, slowly letting your eyes wander over someone else, they will be able to tell that you are interested in them.
- **The lips:** When it comes to the body language of attraction, there is one common sign that works for most people—the lips. The lips are usually slightly parted when someone is looking at someone that they are attracted to, and you can use this cue yourself to show that to someone that you want to attract. You may see that they are standing in that same position. Try licking your lips—just slightly and barely noticeably—if they return the gesture, they are probably interested in you. If not, you can make them more open to the idea with that lick of the lips.
- **The eyes on the lips:** Also make sure that you look closely at the other person's lips. When you look at them, you may get the other person interested in giving you a kiss. The eyes down at the lips are one of the clearest signs of attraction that you can give to other people and if you can do so, you will find that they may actually be just as interested in you.
- **The fleeting, "accidental" touch:** When you brush up against someone "accidentally" while absolutely intending

to do so, you can actually begin to attract them. You can get them into the mood and bring out the attraction just by making sure that you do this. Especially if they are already interested in you, this is a great way for you to begin trying to bring them closer than ever.

CONCLUSION

And with that, you have made it to the end of *Manipulation*. Hopefully, as you read through this book, you found that you were provided with everything that you would need to know about how you can begin to influence other people. Remember, in reading through this book, you were given many different ways that you could begin to influence the behaviors of other people. You have scratched the surface of many different methods that exist and many different ways that you can use to control other people. You have been shown a world that you can use to your own advantage if you know what you are doing, and if you know how to do so, you can begin to influence just about anyone in your life. You can learn to influence people with ease using this just so you are better able to take control.

You were guided through all sorts of ways that you can begin to control other people. You are now aware of all of the ways that the human mind is surprisingly fragile and endlessly able to be infiltrated. The human mind is far from secure and nothing makes that more apparent than many of the ways that people can be perfectly simply manipulated, all by changing the way that you act and by the way that you choose to approach them.

Remember that behind all of these processes is the use of a simple principle: Thoughts lead to feelings and feelings lead to behaviors, which again lead to more thoughts. If you want to be able to control other people, you must remind yourself that, at the end of the day, you are in control. You must remind yourself that you need to be able to step in and alter that cycle within people. Remember that you must always keep yourself hidden so you know that you will not be spotted by other people. Remember that you must always do your best to ensure that, at the end of the day, you are able to control the ways that you behave, and in controlling those behaviors, you allow yourself better control over others as well.

From here, all that is left for you to keep in mind is the idea that you must only manipulate other people if you are willing and able to pay the price. Do not influence the minds of other people if you have no interest in taking responsibility for what you have done. Do not influence the minds of people if you are not sure what the end result will be. Keep in mind that, at the end of the days, you do remember that messing with people and their minds can be quite dangerous and you will need to remember that point. As you use these methods that you have been provided, make sure that you remember to consider what the aftermath could be if you make use of these methods. Remind yourself of the ways that you could see some very real change if you were to use these methods in other ways. Make sure that you remind yourself that ultimately, you control the ways that you interact and you are responsible for the end result.

Thank you for taking the time to read this book and thank you for making it to the end. If you have found that this book has been useful to you, please consider heading over to Amazon today to leave a review!

HOW TO ANALYZE
PEOPLE

Using Emotional Intelligence to Analyze People

NADINE WATSON

INTRODUCTION

Welcome to *How to Analyze People* and thank you for downloading. In this book we are going to examine a number of ways in which you can analyze people and how to do so. To begin, we will look at why you may wish to analyze people in the first place. Then, we will look at the skill of analyzing people and some tips for doing so before you begin reading the first chapter of this book. Then, we will look at what this book will go over so that you know what you can expect to gain through reading it.

Why Analyze People?

You may be wondering to yourself, "why would I want to know how to analyze people?" There are a number of answers to this question, all which support the fact that you should read this book now and not wait any longer! Through being able to analyze people, you have a lot to gain.

Have you ever gotten a "bad feeling" about someone but you weren't sure of why this was? Have you ever deemed someone to be untrustworthy, but you couldn't find the words to explain it? Have you ever met someone for the first time and felt a genuine connection to them, but you didn't know why this was? The answers to all of these situations and many, many more are explained through understanding how to analyze people.

You can analyze people without saying a word to them, and some of us are able to do this innately. All of us know how to analyze people to some degree, but there are some people who already have a strong natural ability to analyze others. This natural ability is closely tied to a person's level of emotional intelligence. Emotional intelligence means being able to understand other people's emotions and take a look at things from their perspective, as well as being able to understand your own emotions. People with a high level of emotional intelligence are better able to analyze people as they are very good at putting themselves int eh shoes of others in order to better understand them. One way that you can test your own level of emotional intelligence before we begin examining it in depth in this book is by assessing your own body language and your ability to empathize with other people. Are you a person that often understands how others are feeling? Do you understand your own emotions? Or are you someone that is always confused as to how other people feel? Do you have trouble looking at something from another person's point of view? This is all crucial when it comes to analyzing people. You will get to learn more about these topics throughout this book. Analyzing people is what allows us to form first impressions of them, and as you know, some people are better at this than others.

First impressions are a very valid and telling look into a person and their character, and mostly all of the information that you can gain from first impressions is due to your ability to pick up on subtle cues that other humans exhibit which give us information. You will learn much more about these subtle clues throughout this book, and this may shed some light on your feelings toward certain people after only meeting them once.

Analyzing people can come in handy in a variety of scenarios such as the following,

- You are a sales person and you want to analyze a potential client in order to strategize your pitch
- You want to start building more meaningful connections with people, so you want to find the right type of people to build friendships and relationships with
- You are an employer looking to hire new staff and you want to ensure you are choosing the right people
- You are meeting your daughter's boyfriend for the first time and you want to make sure his intentions are pure
- And many, many others…

Regardless of your reason why, what these situations all have in common is that you need to understand a person's body language, personality type and communication style in order to get a strong read on them from your very first meeting. These first meetings are often short, so you must hone your analytical skills in order to get a strong read from the very first time you meet them. Further, at the most basic level of analyzing others, it is important to learn how to read people in order for you to know how to approach them. If you are looking to get directions from a stranger on the street, you may be reading their body language to find someone that appears more friendly so you can ask them for directions. You would want to be able to read the body language of someone who looks unhappy or angry as that is a person you may not want to approach in the middle of the street. It is also important to be able to read people you already have relationships with. If a friend looks unhappy, you may want to have a conversation about why they are feeling down. By understanding people and being able to read unspoken messages can help you be a better friend, significant other, or coworker.

Analyzing People As A Skill

One of the most important skills to learn in life is the ability to analyze others. By learning to read people better, you are able to advance your life in a variety of different areas.

- In your professional life

If you are seeking a promotion from your boss, you may be able to read their body language, verbal and non-verbal messages, and their overall mood in order to determine if it's the right time to ask for a promotion or a raise. Or at a lower level, you can determine what more they want to see from you in order for you to gain a promotion.

- In your dating life and romantic relationships

If there is someone that you're romantically interested in, being able to analyze them properly will allow you to get an understanding of what your relationship with them is like in their eyes. By being able to assess the level and strength of your relationship, you may be better able to ask them out on a date or to initiate more conversations with them without risking embarrassment.

- In your friendships and social life

If you are meeting new people who are potential friends, being able to analyze them and form accurate first impressions about what kind of people they are will help you to determine if they are people who you feel that you will get along with, or if they are people who are better kept at a distance. This will help you to avoid possible drama down the line.

Not only are there numerous benefits to learning how to analyze people but being able to analyze a person allows you to tailor your own communication style in order to properly read and match the other people whom you are interacting with. This allows you to grow closer with people and to build more rapport with them, and it develops your levels of social awareness as well. This takes skill and practice, and throughout this book you will learn how to develop this skill to make it as strong as possible. Learning to tailor your communication and entire demeanor to match the situation and the relationship that you have with that person is crucial when it comes to finding the right tone with which to speak and the right words to say. However, in order to do this, you must be able to analyze the person accurately first.

For example, if you notice that your boss looks unhappy, stressed, and angry one day, and you determine this by assessing his facial expression and posture, that may not be the best day to approach him with a 3-week vacation request that day. Most people who are able to read the situation and the person they are interacting with will choose another day where their boss is in a better mood to ask for a favor. This comes down to the skill of being able to analyze a person and read the situation as a whole.

What This Book Will Cover

This book will teach you the tools and skills needed to assess anyone you want so you can find the right moments to ask for what you need and to further your desired relationships. I will start off by teaching you the fundamentals of nonverbal communication. Since nonverbal communication makes up 60% of a person's overall communication, understanding aspects like body language and facial expressions will help you better control your own communication and also help you better assess others. Once you've got a grasp on nonverbal communication, we will move onto learning about verbal communication. In this chapter, you will learn the differences between 'listening' and 'hearing' which will help you better understand others. I will also touch on other topics such as helping you learn to analyze other people's verbal communication. After this, I will teach you the topic of emotional intelligence. This is extremely important in analyzing people as a person with low EI will struggle a lot in understanding other people's feelings and thoughts. Training your EI to be at a high level will help you get a better grasp on other people's thoughts and emotions. Once we've covered this, I will move onto teaching you techniques to help you identify when you are being lied to. One of the main reasons why people want to learn how to analyze people is to figure out if the other person is lying. Most people are bad liars so this is actually a really easy thing to do as long as you recognize the right signs.

Towards the end of this book, I will teach you about the different personality types that exist. Understanding these will help you understand the common archetypes of people out there. It will help you be able to put two and two together and figure out what type of a person the person you're analyzing is. Next, we will spend some time studying your own body language. This is extremely important as many people convey very specific messages using their body language and being able to control that will help you send the right message to people. In the last chapter of this book, I will be combining all topics to help you put everything together.

The only thing more important about understanding these topics is your ability to practice them repeatedly. Only with practice would you be able to notice patterns in a person's body language and be able to figure out their own unique communication style. You may not be able to read a stranger very well at first but practicing on people you know can help you figure out which areas you should be looking out for. Without further ado, let's dive right in.

NONVERBAL COMMUNICATION

NONVERBAL COMMUNICATION IS the main aspect of which people base their first impressions on. Due to this fact, it is crucial that we build a goo understanding of what our body language comes off as to other people. By doing this, we can better understand other people's body language thus, helping us analyze them. Typically, you can learn a lot about a person without even having to speak a single word to them simply by just analyzing their body language and facial expressions. We do this already in our day to day life simply because we are visual creatures. Our eyes perceive the world around us, and this is no different when perceiving people. Learning what to look for and how to decipher this type of communication involves fine-tuning a skill that each of us already possesses. You can almost quickly profile anybody just by assessing their nonverbal communication skills. This chapter will teach you about the basics of nonverbal communication and what each body part/movement means.

. . .

*W*hat Does Nonverbal Communication Mean?

Before we dive into the details of body language, what does nonverbal communication actually mean? This term defines the different ways that people can communicate without the use of words. This involves things that people do (or do not do) that send messages about what they think and feel. People typically are very careful when it comes to sharing information with other people. They will make an effort to choose who and when they will share certain information with, but their bodies will give them away if it is not in line with what they are saying. This type of physical, bodily communication can be either a conscious or unconscious action, meaning that we may not even know that we are sharing our thoughts, feelings or opinions in ways other than through our words. It is important to understand this concept because of what messages you may be sending and also because of what others may be saying without being aware of it.

*D*ifferent Types Of nonverbal Communication

Now, let's take a look at the various different types of nonverbal communication and learn about what they could be telling you about a person. This is the first step in learning to analyze a person. I have made a list for you to simplify things, study this thoroughly as these are the types of cues you should look out for in yourself and others when it comes time for practice.

1. FACIAL EXPRESSIONS

The first type of body language cue I will be teaching you about are facial expressions. From the time we are infants, we are able to see and read facial expressions. The faces our parents made to make us laugh or the faces they made when they were unhappy with us. As babies, we are attuned to the facial expressions of our caregivers as we are nonverbal creatures at this age. Into adulthood though, facial expressions are still a very trustworthy and sometimes not-so-subtle way of reading a person. The faces people make when sad, happy, angry or afraid are universal- they are innately human and do not vary among cultures or languages. Learning to control your own facial expressions will allow you to convey the message you want to deliver, whether you actually mean it or not. On the other hand, learning to analyze them on other people will allow you to get a more accurate read on how this person is feeling and what thoughts are going on in their mind.

2. Eye Contact

The next type of body language we will look at is visual communication. The eyes are usually the place we look when we are having a face to face interaction with someone. The eyes can tell so much about one's thoughts and feelings. The actions they take, such as how long they will hold our gaze if they will even make eye contact at all, or how often they are blinking can give us information about what is going on behind them. Later on, in this book, I will dive deeper into different eye movements and gazes and what they could mean.

3. Hand Gestures

Gestures are deliberate signals or movements that are done to convey a message. These can be used to replace verbal communication on purpose. Think of the signals you may use to communicate a message when you are in a very loud place or when you are trying to communicate to someone without letting the other people in earshot know what you are saying.

4. SPACE

Space is the next type of nonverbal communication we will discuss. This can vary greatly between societies, but in general, you can determine how someone feels in your presence and about what you are saying by how much space they leave between you and them. In some cultures, it is normal to stand very close to someone when you are speaking to them, and in others that would be considered very intrusive. The key here, however, is to know what the individual person's default amount of distance would be and use that as a guide. Many times, when you are immersed in an unfamiliar culture, you may think that someone is being 'rude' or too 'touchy' when simply they may just have a different cultural norm of space.

5. TOUCH

Another form of body language similar to space, is touch. Touch varies greatly between societies and cultures but in any case, we as humans respond to touch. Sometimes touch will indicate that someone is empathizing with what you are saying, and they are breaking the space barrier between you in order to show you that they are supportive. Sometimes the person feels comfortable with you and they will use touch as a gesture to communicate a certain point in a story or explanation. On the flip side of this though, sometimes touch is used in a more negative context. Sometimes touch is used to demonstrate power or superiority. People will sometimes place their hand on your shoulder or on your head as a way of saying that they are above you and are in control of you. People may use touch in order to force something they wish by taking an object from your hand or physically moving you out of their way.

Touch is a form of nonverbal communication that can demonstrate either extreme closeness or extreme distance and disdain. The way that it is done will demonstrate very different messages. An example of this is at the beginning of a relationship, where the first instance of touch is a nonverbal way of sending a big message. On a date, the first time someone takes your hand or puts their arm around you will tell you how they feel about you instantly without a word from their mouth. To that point though, it can also work in the reverse. On a date, if the other person keeps their distance by staying at arm's length and avoiding touch completely, this can tell you that they likely are not interested in pursuing anything further.

From the time we are young, our parents use touch to show us they love us. They may also use touch to show us that we have been bad by spanking us on the behind. A simple touch can contain an immense amount of information.

6. Vocal Dynamics

You may be thinking that vocal dynamics may fall under verbal communication, however, there is a whole lot more to a message than just the words in it. The way that someone delivers a sentence is much more telling than the words it contains. For example, the inclusion of a pause or a drawn-out word and even complete silence can tell you about a person's internal state. If a person becomes suddenly silent, they may be offended by the topic of conversation or by something that was said. If the person avoids silence at all costs, they are likely a nervous or anxious person who is uncomfortable with a silent moment or two. The tone of voice and volume play a huge part in this as well. If you didn't understand a word that someone was saying but could read their verbal communication cues, you would be able to tell a lot about what they were trying to convey. Like facial expressions, this is another type of nonverbal communication that we learn when we are very young. We can tell the difference between a happy and an angry sentence even before we have a full vocabulary to use and understand the meaning of the sentence. The volume of a person's voice can also indicate traits of their personality or their current state. If they are speaking very quietly, they are probably shy or nervous, while a loud volume can mean that they are angry or excited. A great example of the tone of a person's voice demonstrating more than what their words are saying is sarcasm. When we are using sarcasm, the tone of our voice is exactly the opposite of what we are saying. The message we are trying to convey is not evident in the words we are saying, but rather the tone in which we are saying them. If someone were to misunderstand our tone, they would become very confused as to what we meant. If we say, "I loved waiting in line for four hours", the tone we say it with indicates that we actually mean exactly the opposite.

7. APPEARANCE

Personal Appearance is a type of nonverbal communication that takes place more in the conscious mind than some others we have discussed. This type, however, is still important to note as it aids in forming a first impression of a person, especially from afar. The colors people choose to wear, the types of garments they choose and the level of perceived effort or time one has put into their outward appearance all play into our analysis of them. For instance, if you seem someone that is dressed in all black, metal chains, spikes, dark make up and a mohawk hairstyle, you may assume that they are unfriendly. However, if you speak to this person, you may find out that it may actually be the opposite. The way you shape your appearance and the way others choose to appear plays a huge role in what you think of them and how others will think of you.

8. Energetic Changes

The next type of nonverbal communication that we will examine is Energy or energetic changes that a person's body may give off. This type is different from the previously discussed varieties as it is not a classically regarded form of nonverbal communication. If you have ever felt that there was something causing you to feel uncomfortable or awkward in a situation or a room where nobody has spoken and where there are no signs of body language telling you there is something going on in other people's minds, this could be the type of energy we are talking about. There are places within our bodies that actually create electrical signals such as the heart and the neurons in our brains. While the concept of energy is a relatively novel one within the psychology field, it is no doubt they're in our bodies. There may be a type of nonverbal communication that we can pick up on from others' bodies that makes us feel certain ways in response. Some use the term 'vibe' to explain the things we feel but cannot see and have a difficult time explaining with words.

9. Bodily Changes

A type of nonverbal communication that is completely out of our control is the bodily changes that happen when we feel certain emotions. Some people may turn red in the face when they are embarrassed. Some may begin shaking when they are enraged, and some people's eyes widen, and their pupils dilate. When we have a sudden rush of fear or feel threatened, we have an automatic bodily response that is caused by the release of adrenaline. This happens automatically to all of us and dates back to our days as early humans and cavemen. When we were hunter-gatherers and had to live outdoors and hunt our own food, we were constantly threatened by the potential danger of predators, natural disasters or enemy tribes. Because of this, we needed to have a natural instinct to save ourselves. If you have ever heard of the term fight or flight, this concept is what it is in reference to. When we feel afraid, our body responds by causing our pupils to dilate, our bodies to stiffen, heart rate to increase and our breathing to change. All of these responses are to prepare us to face the issue causing us to be afraid. These days in modern society, we do not need to rely on these body changes nearly as much, but they still occur. We may be used to noticing these responses in ourselves, and this will help us to know what to look for in others. If you give someone news that makes them afraid, you will likely notice the changes in their body that communicate their feelings.

Sweating is another nonverbal communication that happens auto-matically. This may be a sign of nerves and is often visible on people's brow, upper lip or even sometimes through their shirt at their underarms. Another type of feeling that may cause physiolog-ical changes is sadness. For some, we will begin tearing up when we become saddened and this happens automatically. These responses are all of an emotional nature and our emotions are virtually impossible to control and quite hard to fake.

10. ACTUAL BODY LANGUAGE

The next and final type of communication is body language. Body language is a fairly broad term and can include several of the previously discussed forms of nonverbal communication such as gestures and facial expressions, but it can also include things such as touch and head movements. This can mean the way you are standing, your body movements or where you place your arms during a conversation can all add up to form a nonverbal impression. A person standing with their arms crossed sends a less friendly message to you when compared to someone who may be standing with their arms to the side. We will look at this in much more detail in the following section. Body language can be conscious or unconscious. For the purposes of analyzing people however, it is helpful to focus more heavily on the unconscious type as it will be much more telling when a person does not even realize the messages that their body is portraying to other people in an interaction.

*W*hat Is Body Language?

Now that you know more about nonverbal communication, we are going to look at body language in more detail. Body language is a term which overlaps with nonverbal communication in many ways, as it is an umbrella term that encompasses many different ways that people communicate using their body instead of their words. Body language is a form of nonverbal communication that includes many different parts of the body. We will look at some examples as well as how to read what they could be telling you about a person or about an interaction or encounter.

Understanding body language is an invaluable tool in being able to analyze people. Body language is a very broad term and can encompass many different things. To better understand what it means, think of the first few times you had a conversation with someone over a form of technology like text messaging. We have all surely had misunderstandings over text message conversations because we misinterpreted something the other person said to us, or they thought we were angry with them. These problems happen because we do not have anything but their words to interpret. There is no tone of voice, no eye contact, no facial expressions and no posture to read. Now think of how different it is when you are face to face with someone, having a conversation with them. Think of how many more factors there are to take into account when they are standing in front of you. All of these added factors are forms of body language and nonverbal communication. We barely notice that all of this is going on in our interactions because we are so used to it. it is only when it is all taken away and we have a misunderstanding via text messaging that we notice how important and communicative body language is in our lives and our relationships.

*M*ore On Body Language

As you can understand, body language plays a part in every interaction we have, and this is why it is so important to understand. We have been observing it all our lives, but we may not have been aware. Having an awareness of what you are seeing and picking up on will give you insight into why you may feel a certain way about a person, whether positive or negative. The cues as to why you feel a certain way about a person are likely in their body language.

*A*s I mentioned when I first introduced the concept of body language in the previous section, body language can be either conscious or unconscious. The majority of us are very familiar with conscious body language as we more than likely use this as a form of communication on a regular basis. An example of a conscious display of body language are hand signals. These vary between cultures and regions of the world, but every culture has some. They may change with changes in pop culture, or they may be long-standing such as the thumbs up in North America. These hand signals are a form of body language that we use to convey specific messages to others. Another example is a handshake. A handshake is a nonverbal way of saying that you are welcoming someone to make contact with you and is a friendly greeting upon meeting someone new. Another example of conscious body language are facial expressions. There are many facial expressions that we consciously make in order to convey messages to people. Facial expressions can convey anger, sadness or happiness. Humans often make these facial expressions to tell others how they feel without speaking. Have you ever been with your partner in a situation where they said something that frustrated you and you gave them a look to let them know that they will be hearing about it when you are alone later? With this one simple facial expression, they know what is to come.

For the remainder of this section, we will focus on the more subtle and more nuanced type of body language which are called *unconscious displays of body language*. We can gain more valuable information from this type of body language for the following reason. Any person can consciously put out an image to the world that represents how they wish to be perceived. This is how each person wishes to be seen and is put forth consciously. This is the type of outward expression that we would read from people if we took all of their actions at face value. However, it takes skill and knowledge to look for and decode the subtle, unconscious messages that people do not realize they are conveying through their body language. There are hints that we will learn to look for that will tell us what a person is really thinking or feeling, as well as whether or not it is something different from what they are saying or actively trying to show. You will get a better understanding of this in the next section.

How To Read Body Language Cues And Figure Out What They Mean

Before we begin looking at specific body language cues, it is important to note that in an interaction with another person, even a completely nonverbal interaction, many of these nonverbal communications and cues will be happening at the same time. These all work together to give you an impression or a reading of the person you are interacting with. For example, someone's facial expression coupled with their distance from you can tell you that they may be uncomfortable or upset. We are all dynamic beings and none of these things will happen entirely independently. Keeping this in mind when entering an interaction with another person will aid you in your analysis of them and the things that they are telling you without saying a word.

We will now begin to look at unconscious body language by studying different areas of the body. We will examine all of these different areas of the body and what they may be telling us by their different actions.

Facial Body Language

The face is where we will begin. The face is very involved when it comes to deciphering nonverbal communication because it has so much to tell us. There are many different places to look for clues on the face. The first one we will discuss is the eyes.

1. THE EYES

Firstly, we are going to look at the eyes. Our eyes operate greatly on their own accord- blinking when they need to and gazing where there is movement. While we can most often control where they look, they will sometimes operate on their own in interactions with others. The eyes will often be the first place to show how the person is feeling. Our brain and our spinal cord make up the pairing that is known as the central nervous system. This pathway of neurons operates fully automatically- that is to say, with no help from our conscious mind. The eyes are connected to this nervous system and are the only part of the central nervous system that actually faces the outside of the body. Because of this, the eyes are literally intertwined with what we are thinking and feeling, even more than we notice. The brain and the spinal cord give us life-they are responsible for initiating our movements, our thoughts, and our feelings. "The eyes are the window to the soul" got its origins in this fact of anatomy. That being said, it is very difficult to control the emotions and sentiments that people can see in our eyes as they come directly from the places within us over which we have no control. The eyes, therefore, are the first place to look when it comes to seeing someone's truth.

*E*ye contact is a big indicator of the intentions of a person. As previously discussed, the amount of eye contact someone is making is an indicator of their level of comfort. If someone is making and holding eye contact for a long period of time without looking away, they appear to be very comfortable to the point of seeming like they may have predeter-mined intentions. If someone is avoiding eye contact altogether, they tend to seem very untrustworthy, almost as if they are trying very hard to hide something from you. We have all encountered an uncomfortable amount of eye contact, whether too much or too little, where it made us feel like something was not right. You may have been feeling unease but were unaware as to why. Feeling someone's eyes staring directly into yours with no end in sight makes for a lot of discomfort while trying to catch someone's eye who is clearly making an effort to avoid yours makes for a very awkward conversation. If someone is making steady eye contact, looking away every now and then and then coming back to meet your eyes once again, they are probably feeling comfortable in the situation or conversation and are quite secure with themselves and their position. This amount of eye contact makes us feel comfortable in the other person's presence and feel that their intentions are pure.

*E*ye movement is also a type of communication that goes on. The eyes tend to go where the person wants to go. If someone glances at something, chances are they are thinking about it or wishing to go there. For example, if someone glances at a chair in the room, they are probably tired of standing. If someone glances at the door, they would probably like to leave or may be late for something. If you see someone looking over at another table for the duration of your dinner date, chances are they are wishing they were with someone else. Think of yourself in this type of situation. On a date where you feel bored and unenthused, you would probably be searching wildly around the room for an excuse to leave or another person to daydream about. If your date is unaware of what your eye movements are demonstrating, they may keep droning on about the stock market for another hour or two.

*W*hile everyone blinks at slightly different rates, you can start to pick up on changes in blinking speed. Watch your partner next time they are sitting across from you and notice how often they blink. Picking up on this will alert you when there is a change in blinking speed. Blinking very often and quickly is said to be an indicator of thinking hard or of stress. What causes your partner to begin blinking quickly? This observation will give you some insight into what causes them stress and mental strain.

2. THE MOUTH

Another place to look on the face is the mouth. The mouth's subtle movements often go completely unnoticed by the person them- selves. We will examine a smile for instance. A genuine smile will include a change or movement in all parts of the face, this happens automatically and is not controlled by the person. A fake smile, however, will only involve the movement of the mouth into the desired shape of a smile and not involve the eyes or the upper areas of the face. These two types of smiles can tell a great deal about what a person is thinking. A real and genuine smile indicates that the person is happy and interested, while a fake smile indi- cates that the person wants approval or acceptance. Another type of smile is one that includes the movement of only one side of the mouth. This type indicates that the person is feeling unsure or not convinced.

3. THE FACE AS A WHOLE

Subtle movements of the face can be picked up when examining another person closely. These subtle movements are said to happen instinctively when a person has a feeling of intense emotion. They are very difficult to fake as they happen quickly and subtly. These subtle movements can be very telling if we can learn to pick up on them.

The first involuntary facial movement is that of surprise. When genuinely surprised, a human face will drop the jaw, raise the eyebrows and widen the eyes. The second is fear.

Fear causes the eyebrows to rise slightly, the upper eyelid to raise and the lips to tense. The next is disgust, which causes the upper lip to rise and the nose to wrinkle. Anger causes the eyebrows to lower, the lips to come together and the bottom jaw to come forward. Happiness causes the corners of the lips to rise, the cheeks to rise and the outsides of the eyes to wrinkle. This wrinkling of the eyes is indicative of a real smile, as in a fake smile this does not happen. Sadness involves the outside of the lips to lower, the inside of the eyebrows to raise and the lower lip to come forward. Finally, an intense feeling of hate causes one side of the mouth to raise. These expressions all take place so quickly that they are often missed. If you know what to look for though, you will notice them before they are gone. This will be one of the most accurate ways to analyze a person as they will likely have no idea that this has occurred on their face.

The face has a lot to say when it comes to body language, and with so many small muscles there are a lot of movements that occur unbeknownst to the person being observed. This is a great place to start when it comes to learning to analyze people.

Reading the language of the rest of the body can be better understood when done from the perspective of looking at an animal. Animals' main priority is always to protect themselves if a fight were to occur. They always have their vital areas covered when they are in a vulnerable position or situation and will open up when they feel safe. Humans are similar in this way. Our vital areas are all in the middle of our body- around our heart and lungs. When we see an animal in a strange setting or around other animals that it may have to fight with it will be positioned in a way where nothing will be able to access its heart, its lungs or its stomach area. Thinking of humans in this way will be a great tool for analyzing them.

The Body

Now we will look at other areas of the body and the messages we can get from learning how to read them accurately.

1. THE ARMS

First, is the movement of the arms. The arms themselves can close us off or open us up to the world. The positioning of the arms in relation to the body can be something that happens automatically. Someone may be extremely comfortable with the situation they are in if they have their arms at their sides, resting on the armrests of the chair in which they are seated. This may happen automatically as a result of feeling unthreatened and safe in their surroundings.

A person may cross their arms when they are feeling threatened or hug their chest in an effort to protect themselves from the outside world. When people do this they are attempting to physically put a barrier between themselves and you, whether they know this to be true or not. Our bodies are made to automatically protect us from danger. Our emotions and feelings signal to our body that there may be a threat and our body acts accordingly. This happens regardless of whether there is a real physical threat, or simply a topic of conversation that is making us uncomfortable. to our brain, it is all the same. When someone is feeling comfortable and welcoming, they may open their arms and leave themselves fully open to receiving the world.

. . .

*A*rms behind the back indicate that the person is feeling secure and welcoming a challenge. We know this because they have their protecting elements (their arms) behind them and their chest out and exposed meaning that they will not be able to quickly protect themselves if need be. This is an indication of feeling secure and comfortable or feeling like they are stronger than those around them.

2. THE HANDS

The hands being up around the face indicates a desire to remain mysterious or not to show one's true expressions.

*H*ands on hips may indicate that a person is trying to assert dominance. When someone puts their hands on their hips, it makes them take up much more space. Putting the hands on the hips is usually accompanied by a wide stance. This type of body positioning causes people to spread themselves out as if to say, "you can try to cross me but it will not work".

*H*ands in the pockets can indicate nervousness and even deceitful behavior as they are hiding a part of themselves that tends to move in an indicative way. Look out for this along with other signals that the person may be trying to withhold information or remain vague.

*T*he hands holding something between the person, and you create another type of barrier like crossing the arms does. For example, holding a book or a notepad out in front of them is putting something between themselves and you in order to distance themselves from the conversation. this can indicate unease or a lack of openness which can translate to their words being distant or reserved.

3. The Feet

The feet are another important place to look in order to analyze a person. This is because people are usually expecting their face to be the place people look to for clues into their subconscious, so they forget all about their feet placement. The feet placement is similar to the glance mentioned earlier in that it tells you where the person wants to be. Just as someone will glance in the direction of what they want, their feet will usually point in the direction of where they want to be. If someone is talking to you but their feet are pointing to the restroom, they may be trying to find a moment to exit and take care of their business. If their feet are pointing at someone else, chances are they would rather be talking to them. If their feet are pointing to you, they are engaged in your conversation and would not rather be elsewhere at that moment. This can tell you about someone's intentions and paired with their facial expression or arm placement, you can determine their motives.

4. Body Accessories and Ornaments

Another way that people demonstrate their internal happenings without speaking is the ornaments or accessories they choose. This is another way we can analyze someone before we even speak to them. Examples of this include clothing, jewelry, and hairstyle choices. These choices communicate information about the wearer. A tight, slick or pulled back hairstyle communicates profession- alism and seriousness, while a loose, flowing hairstyle communicates a laid-back attitude. Think of the classic surfer image versus the business look. Even the clothing is very different between these two examples. A surfer will wear baggier, brighter clothing while business executives wear muted tones and tighter fitting clothes. At first encounter, we automatically assume very different things about the personality traits or attitudes of these two people because we have been seeing these differences for our entire lives.

To examine this point regarding accessories and ornaments even further, the way that people use and interact with their accessories is another thing to look for. Someone who is playing with one of their accessories while speaking to you or waiting for something can be said to seem anxious and on edge or nervous. Someone who is wearing their accessories but has seemingly forgotten their existence comes across as someone very comfortable and secure in themselves.

5. THE INTERACTION WITH THE ENVIRONMENT

The way that someone interacts with their external environment can often be overlooked but can tell us a great deal about how this person is feeling. Similar to how they interact with their accessories, someone who will not sit still or who is pacing indicates that they are feeling stressed or nervous. Someone who taps their foot or shakes their leg nonstop throughout an interaction with you is demonstrating some type of unease and anxious behavior. We can take these types of body movements to mean that the person is feeling some degree of discomfort. This can be a starting point for our analysis as it is quite obvious body language. Know that a person is uneasy or feeling nervous can create the basis for our examination of them.

· · ·

*T*he way we sit is often taught to us when we are young children- sitting 'properly' means that we are sitting straight up with our legs facing forward and our feet on the floor. We carry this into adult life and can observe the way other adults sit in order to analyze them. When we are children, we are scolded for sitting with our feet on the couch or chair, with our elbows on the table or slouching. Seeing this type of body language in adults can indicate disrespect or being unconcerned with politeness.

*H*ow To Read A Person

You may now be wondering how this information about body language cues is known since every person is different from one another. This is true, no two people are exactly alike, and everyone has their own unique resting state.

*T*he key when looking for clues in body language is to notice where and when the changes occur. If someone is blinking at regular speed, until someone new joins the conversation and then they begin blinking at an increased rate, this may be an indication that the person is attracted to them or has a crush on them. We can look for things such as this to give us more clues about what the body language might be telling us by changes in a situation that occurred around the same time as changes in body language. Was there a change in a topic that seemed to make a person cross their arms or begin fidgeting with their tie? Neither of these may seem particularly relevant on their own, but when coupled they are much more telling. Further, the time that they occur tells us even more about the situation as well as comparing the changing of states of the person over the course of the interaction.

*F*actors That Influence Body Language

There are many factors that come into play when you are reading body language. In this section, we will discuss some things to look out for when analyzing a person's body language, as it could be attributed to one of these factors, or one of these factors may be influencing the person's actions.

1. GENDER

As you may have imagined, gender plays a role in body language. In most societies around the world, men and women are raised quite differently. This translates into differences in social status, the likelihood of certain career choices, and differences in body language. In general, men tend to be more comfortable than women taking up space in the world. Many women are less comfortable spreading themselves out in spaces and will more often make themselves smaller to take up less space in the world. Men also tend to be bigger than women in their shoulders and their height, so they will naturally take up more space regardless. Men tend to is sit with their legs spread wide while women usually sit with their legs crossed or their knees together. Knowing this general difference will avoid confusion when we analyze someone. If a woman regularly sits with her legs wider, notice when this changes. If a man normally sits with his knees spread very wide, notice when he makes himself smaller. What was being discussed, what was going on around him? Knowing when these things change is the key to analyzing the genders and their spatial volume. This is similar to if a man has his chest and shoulders spread, he is not necessarily attempting to appear confident and dominant because he could naturally have a wider chest and shoulders. If we can observe the man's regular width and posture, we can observe when he is spreading himself out, even more, to appear confident. These changes may be more easily noticed in women however they are still there for us to observe in men only slightly less apparent.

*I*n a general sense, men tend to be more aggressive in their movements, where women tend to be gentler and softer. When a man performs an aggressive movement such as a handshake, it is helpful to keep in mind that it may just be the fact that men have more testosterone, and this makes them tend towards aggression much more than women. This is not to mean aggression in a negative sense, we are not talking about the type of aggression that is of the intent to harm other people, but a more subtle and general level of aggressive movements specifically.

*A*nother point to note is the voice differences between men and women. Men have much deeper voices than women. Typically, when we listen to a person speak, their tone of voice tells us quite a great deal about how they are feeling. It is worth keeping in mind that men already have a much deeper voice and normally will use a smaller range of tones when they speak. Women, on the other hand, tend to use a wider range of voice tones when they speak. It is helpful to think about this in terms of a person telling a story. When a woman tells a story, she tends to use a wide range of tones depending on the part of the story and what is happening. She will go from very high pitched in moments of excitement, to lower in moments of fear or sadness. A man telling a story will tend to remain closer to his natural tone of voice regardless of what the emotional state of the story is. Analyzing a man's tone of voice may be more difficult than analyzing that of a woman. We must listen for subtle differences when analyzing the changes in the voice of a man, such as a volume and pitch. These differences will likely be much more subtle than that of a woman, but if we can recognize the average resting tone of a man's voice, we will be better able to notice when his voice has changed to a higher or lower tone. This will signal to us that we must look closer and examine other body language signals along with the voice to analyze him.

$\mathcal{F}$acial expressions are another point of difference between the genders. In North American societies, women are raised to be pleasing and agreeable. Because of this, their facial expressions can be read differently than those of men. It may be harder to read a woman's body language because of the difference in expectations placed on the genders from an early age. Women generally smile to demonstrate agreement and non-confrontation. We must not be fooled by thinking that this smile is always telling us about what is really going on. Think back to the facial movements we discussed earlier this chapter. We are now able to decipher a genuine smile from a forced one by looking to the eyes. If you see a woman smiling often throughout your inter-action with her, start looking to the muscles around her eyes to determine if these smiles are coming from the inside thoughts and feelings or not. If the muscles at the outside of her eyes are not engaged but her lips are forming a smile, it is a forced smile and not a genuine one. When does she produce a genuine smile and when does she produce a fake one? Noticing this can give us quite a bit of insight into her personality.

. . .

*K*nowing these gender differences, we can approach conversations and analyses of men and women differently. Just as all individuals are different and have different resting states, men and women are generally different. While there is no rule book for how to analyze men and women differently, just as there is no rule book for analyzing people in general, if we are aware of the differences in regular states of men and women we are better equipped to make an accurate analysis of whoever is in front of us.

2. AGE

Similar to the differences in the body language of the genders, there are notable differences in the body language of different ages. One of these changes is in posture. As we get older, our posture inevitably changes along with the aging of our bones and muscles. Some elderly individuals will have developed a curve in their spine that can lead them to bend forward slightly. This is important to note as it is not to be taken as a sign that they are nervous and timid. They may also be required to sit in a certain way, or to sit more often than they stand. If they choose to sit and it appears to be in a slouched or disinterested manner, this could be because of their health or their body structure that has changed. The bodies of elderly people move differently than the bodies of young and healthy individuals. The way that they demonstrate confidence may be different than a younger person because they simply cannot push out their chest, pull their shoulders back and keep their chin up. They may rely on tone of voice or facial expressions much more to express themselves in a nonverbal way.

· · ·

*A*nother place where these changes can be noticed is in their handshake. Elderly people may not be able to give you a firm and business-like handshake because they are not as strong as they used to be. We must look to other places and techniques we have learned in order to analyze an elderly person by their body language.

3. LEVEL OF COMFORT OR ANXIETY

A person with social anxiety may demonstrate it in a variety of ways, but it will likely be noticeable at first interaction. The body language of a person experiencing social anxiety will include the following; much movement, fidgeting with hair, clothing or accessories, avoiding eye contact, closed-off posture, stiffness, and their feet may be facing the door or the exit route. It may be more difficult to analyze this type of person because all of their body languages may be demonstrating this social unease. If the analysis you are doing is telling you that this person would rather be anywhere but there interacting with you, it may be that they experience anxiety in social situations. In order to proceed to the next step in your analysis of them, you can try to make them feel comfortable and relaxed by demonstrating this the of body language yourself. Matching their body language will lead to an increasingly uncomfortable situation for both parties but being the first one to appear calm and relaxed will indicate to them that their social anxiety is not making you want to leave the situation or avoid them. Showing them this may lead to them feeling more comfortable and in turn, you will be able to see the person behind the fear.

4. TECHNOLOGY

There are new introductions of artificial intelligence every day and with that, the removal of human interaction from many industries and processes throughout our day. Artificial intelligence is not concerned with body language and tone of voice, so how will this affect our natural tendency to read people? As we are such social creatures, we will never be able to fully erase human interaction from our lives. There will always be people we are interacting with on a daily basis and removing the human interaction from some industries such as the fast-food industry or banking may actually leave us with more time to interact with our friends, family, and coworkers because with technology comes efficiency. The advent of technology and its growing replacement of many of our points of human contact with others may have the opposite effect than many people anticipate. This may make reading body language even more important as we will have much more time to do so in inter-actions that matter to our future.

VERBAL COMMUNICATION

Now that you have learned all about nonverbal communication including body language, the next step is to delve into the verbal side of communication. Verbal communication is also important when it comes to analyzing people, as listening comes into play here.

Verbal communication is the type which is used between people that uses words and sounds. This is the type of communication we use when we are meeting someone for the first time or learning more about a person over coffee. This type of communication involves language and dynamics of speech. Verbal communication is innate to humans, as we are all built to learn and use language to communicate with other humans.

This form of communication can become quite complicated when looked at in-depth. Think about sarcasm for example, and how when using sarcasm, you are saying one thing but meaning the exact opposite. For example, "this is fun" when said in a sarcastic tone actually means "this is no fun at all." It takes skill in communication to use and understand this type of verbal communication. The most important components of verbal communication are the actual words that are spoken and the tone of voice that it's said in. Tone of voice is more important than the actual words said. Just like the sarcasm example, you could be saying "Wow, this is great!" but mean the complete opposite. In order to master verbal communication, you must understand how different tones carry entirely different meanings.

$\mathcal{L}$istening As A Type Of Communication

Effective communication with another person comes down to accurately analyzing them. It may be surprising to learn that verbal interpersonal communication is most effective when more emphasis is put on listening to the other person, rather than only on speaking.

$\mathcal{T}$he Importance Of Being A Good Listener

If you are a good communicator, this means you are able to do the following,

- Listen effectively and actively
- Observe your own thoughts and feelings
- Know when a response is not needed
- Observe other people and practice empathy
- Form thoughtful and appropriate responses according to your observations of yourself and others, through empathy

*B*y being able to do all of these things, you are able to connect with people on a deeper level through understanding. You are able to share information with people effectively and receive information as well. These five points are beneficial in all types of relationships. Relationships are all about connection and connection is difficult without the ability to be a good communicator. Listening is one of the most important points on this list and in this section, we are going to look at the importance of being a good listener for those times when effective verbal communication is necessary in helping you to analyze a person.

*W*hy do we want to become a better listener in the first place? Because becoming a better listener means being able to analyze the other person and choose the most effective communication strategy based on this. If you can accurately analyze a person, especially at first encounter, you can determine what communication strategy they will respond to best. For example, if you read someone to be an extrovert, then you will take a light-hearted, familiar approach to a conversation with them. You may make a few jokes to make them feel comfortable because you understand that extroverted people gain energy from others and social interactions. By knowing this and approaching them in this way, you will create a rapport much quicker with them. You would treat the first interaction with someone you deem to be an introvert much differently, however. This is why it is very important to know how to analyze a person. At first interaction with someone who seems to be reserved and shy in a group of people, you can approach them in a quieter way, ensuring not to stand too close or come on too strong. Doing this will make the person feel much more comfortable than if you approached them in the same way as you would approach an introvert. Once you have made either the extrovert or the introvert feel comfortable with you (which you can determine based on reading their body language), they will be more inclined to engage in a conversation with you and open up to you. This is how we can listen to a person even before they have spoken. During the verbal conversation then, you can begin to further analyze them and their personality by listening in the most effective way you can, based on your reading of them.

*I*n the next chapter, we will take this one step further and discuss how to respond in an effective way by choosing your own communication style and body language.

*H*earing Versus Listening

Becoming a better listener requires multiple steps to follow to ensure you are getting the most out of your listening experience. Many times we think we are listening to someone when in reality we are just waiting to respond, or we are thinking of what we will say next for the entire duration of the other person speaking. Does this sound familiar? If we can actively listen with the intent to listen rather than the intent to play our own part in the conversation we can develop a greater understanding of other people. The steps to becoming a better listener are as follows.

Step 1. Listen with the intent to understand rather than the intent to respond.

Listening requires an open mind. If our mind is full of thoughts about how we will respond and what we will say next, then we are unable to really listen and process what we are hearing. We may even think that we are listening, but if we put our thoughts about our response aside and listen closely, the response we would like to give may change drastically from what we would have planned because we have actually understood the person's words before forming a thoughtful response. That is if we deem a response necessary.

Step 2. Tell the person you are hearing them.

There will be appropriate moments in a conversation where you can tell the person that you understand them, that you are hearing them, that you are listening to them. This will make them feel heard and in turn, they will be more inclined to continue sharing their words with you.

Step 3. Ask questions if you need clarification.

If there is something that you simply do not understand after listening intently, it is acceptable to ask for clarification of a specific point or concept. The other person will likely welcome the active listening you are doing, the commitment to understanding and the interest you are showing in what they are saying.

Step 4. Pay attention to what is avoided or left out.

That is to say, read between the lines. If the person only talks about something specific or is obviously avoiding certain topics altogether, this can give you information about them. In some instances, the things people do not say can tell us more about them than what they do say. If we had not been listening very closely, we may not even notice what they left out or we may not remember if they did or did not mention certain things. Listening intently allows you to be sure that they avoided certain things.

Step 5. Decide whether your input is necessary at each point in the conversation.

Sometimes we enjoy hearing ourselves speak and our own opinions, but we are already aware of what our own opinions are. Before contributing to a conversation, briefly determine the intention behind your input. If the intention is to genuinely contribute, then go ahead and do so at the appropriate moment. If the intention, however, is to showcase your knowledge or prove your opinion it may not be necessary to contribute and you may be better off just listening.

Step 6. *Listen* to their body language.

Another very important step to becoming a better listener involves using what we have previously discussed to analyze the person. While listening to someone, analyze their body language and look for clues and insight into how they may be feeling or what they may be thinking. If the person is showing you relaxed body language, like a relaxed sitting posture and arms, open wide, for example, they are comfortable and secure in the conversation. If the person has their arms crossed or is avoiding eye contact, they may be uncomfortable with the topic. More importantly, notice when these body language cues change during an interaction. If the topic changes, do they become suddenly closed-off by putting a barrier like a laptop or a drink between you and them, or do they begin shifting around in their seat? This is an indication that the conversation has reached a topic they are no longer comfortable with. Noticing body language and especially its changes are the key to be a great listener. As you know by now, many of the things that we can interpret from an interaction are the nonverbal things. Listening includes what we observe with our eyes just as much as what we hear.

*H*ow To Analyze Other People's Verbal Communications

In this section, we are going to look at different styles of verbal communication in order to help you analyze a person based on their verbal communication cues. We may all exhibit a combination of all of these different communication styles, but a person can usually be pinned down to one style the majority of the time. Understanding a person's communication style will aid you in being able to receive and understand the communication of others' thoughts and ideas and will help you to understand their nonverbal cues as well. There are four styles of verbal communication that we will examine below.

*T*he first communication style we will explore is the Aggressive Communication Style. This communication style is borne out of a place of fear. This person fears they will not be heard or understood and therefore they enter into interaction or conversation with a loud volume and an attitude of entitlement. They approach the conversation with a wide stance and a confrontational posture. They feel the need to shout over others and force their point of view. This style of communication can often end up having the exact effect the communicator is trying to avoid, which is that people may not end up listening to the content of the sentences because they are distracted by the way that it has been conveyed. When people are faced with an aggressive communication style they tend to become defensive and closed-off, unwilling to engage much further in the interaction.

*T*he second is the Passive/Submissive Communication Style. This type of communicator prefers to avoid conflict at all costs. They would rather please people than to make their opinion known. They are easily swayed and speak with a very low volume. They attempt to shrink themselves down using their body language with hunched shoulders and crossed arms. They feel as if their opinions are not valid and are apologetic if they feel that someone disagrees with them. Other people will approach this type of communicator in an exasperated manner as they feel that they have to walk on eggshells in an effort to preserve the person's feelings.

*T*he next is the Passive-Aggressive Communication Style. These types of communicators initially show one type of attitude on the outside, that their words do not match. They use passive, self-shrinking body language, therefore, appearing to be passive and non-confrontational on the outside, while communicating with their words in an aggressive manner. It is the combination of both of the previous two styles of communication. They tend to speak in an aggressive manner to indirectly make a point but act out passively in front of the person. Their words are of an aggressive nature, but they deliver them in a passive style. They will use a low volume and a gentle tone while saying something that is likely to cause confrontation or to make someone angry. People tend to become frustrated when dealing with this type of communicator because there is a lot of close attention that needs to be paid in order to figure out what exactly they are trying to say.

The final verbal communication style is the Assertive Communication Style. This style of communication is rooted in confidence and self-assuredness. People who communicate in this way have confident body language and maintain eye contact they are relaxed but engaged. They are emphatic but maintain a normal volume and tone of voice. They are secure in their stance both literally and figuratively and are unafraid of rejection or a disagreeing party. They communicate their points with a calm but firm demeanor. This type of communicator is the easiest to communicate with as they are able to remain level-headed in disagreement and are not forceful in any way. They are not trying to enforce an attitude of superiority nor are they trying to remain hidden. They stand in interaction as they are and are not trying too hard to be anything that they are not. People respect the fact that this communicator is able to assert themselves with ease.

As we have learned, communicating with other people involves much more than just speaking. It involves listening well, reading and demonstrating specific body language, analyzing personality types and communicating effectively with your words. A lot goes into a simple conversation and it will take practice to become a great analyzer.

One of the most important things to look out for in analyzing people is being able to be observant and a good listener. By practicing active listening, you will be able to gather a lot of information about someone. If you pair that with observing their body language and facial expressions, you will be able to determine the true meaning of the message they are delivering. For instance, if you are asking a colleague if it's okay that you trade shifts with them, their words may say "Sure, no problem" but their body language and overall demeanor can scream "No!!".

*C*onflicts

At this point in the book you may be wondering how you will know what to say in a situation where you would benefit from using verbal communication and conflict resolution for a situation where you are reading the other person and they are exhibiting hostility. In this case, you may anticipate a conflict, or a conflict may already have begun. In this section, we will look at how to properly and quickly deal with conflict for those times when a person's body language is telling you this will be necessary. Since conflict and arguments are an unavoidable part of life, it is important to learn how to communicate yourself during situations like that. While it may seem like there are a lot of things to remember, it will come more naturally the more you practice it. This subchapter will focus on providing you with techniques and examples on how to express yourself during arguments and conflicts effectively through using proper verbal communication as well as positive body language.

*I*t aims to promote understanding and compassion instead of the hurt and judgment that is usually a result of confrontation. Nonviolent communication diffuses situations even before they become heated and prevents conflicts altogether. By having everyone express themselves through nonviolent communication, situations are resolved well before anger has built up to the point of an outburst.

. . .

*C*onflict is not an inherently negative or violent thing. It does not have to lead to the breakdown of relationships of any kind or yelling and screaming. It does not have to involve a dominant party and a submissive party or an expresser and a listener. Conflict can be seen in a positive way in that it can promote voicing one's thoughts and speaking the truth. This is how situations and relationships can be improved rather than harmed.

*W*hen using nonviolent communication, you are required to look deep within yourself to examine your feelings and your values. What this does is hold every person accountable for what they are actually feeling instead of having everyone cover up what they are feeling with anger and violence. When you use nonviolent communication, you get used to being able to express your feelings in an articulate and clear manner which helps in conflict resolution because everyone is then aware of what you need and what you are not getting. This makes the conflict resolution process much simpler as there is no guesswork involved. Sometimes when there is conflict, you must try to discern what the person needs or wants in order to resolve the conflict, but this is quite difficult because only the person themselves can know this. If they express it to you in simple and clear terms, you don't have to spend the time trying to figure out what it is they need and can instead skip right to the point of resolution. This greatly reduces the chances of miscommunications or misunderstandings which can also be a cause of conflicts getting blown out of proportion or feelings of built up resentment.

· · ·

*T*his type of conflict resolution is not only for co-workers, friends and family but can also be useful in situations where there is conflict between total strangers or when mediation is required between two people who are in conflict. If you understand nonviolent communication, you can use it for a variety of situations with a variety of people, but the common thread is that it leads to peaceful dialogue. It can help to open lines of communication among people who would not otherwise have peaceful dialogue and creates an understanding between them. It is a powerful tool for any situation that you face. In the next chapter, we will look at how you can take charge of your own body language and put forth the messages that you intend to send in specific situations.

HOW TO USE EMOTIONAL INTELLIGENCE TO ANALYZE PEOPLE

IN THIS CHAPTER, we are going to examine the concept of Emotional Intelligence. This concept is very helpful when talking about analyzing people, as emotional intelligence and the ability to analyze people go hand in hand. In this chapter, we will look at what it is and how it will help you in developing your skill or analyzing people.

What Is Emotional Intelligence?

Emotional intelligence is presently defined as a person's ability to recognize, understand and control their emotions. It can also be defined as a person's ability to recognize, understand, and influence the emotions of other people. In the simplest terms, EI is the ability to be aware of the fact that emotions drive human behaviors and have the power to impact other people.

. . .

*E*motional intelligence is made up of the following five components:

- Motivation

*T*hose with high EI tend to have more motivation which makes them to be more optimistic people and have more resilience towards negativity.

- Empathy

*P*eople who are empathetic and compassionate have more success when connecting with others.

- Social skills

A person that has high EI have the social skills that showcase their respect and care for other people. This is why people who have higher EI tend to get along better with most people.

- Self-regulation

*W*hen a person is self-aware, those with high EI are able to regulate their emotions and keep them in check when needed.

- Self-awareness

*W*hen a person has self-awareness, they are able to know their own strengths and weaknesses and have the understanding of how to react properly in situations and to other people.

*H*igh Emotional Intelligence Versus Low Emotional Intelligence

When it comes to the ability to understand your own emotions and the emotions of other people, high emotional intelligence is required. Naturally, a person that has high emotional intelligence are better at communication as they have a good grasp on how others are feeling and how they can properly express their emotions. High emotional intelligence does not mean that someone is always happy or in a positive mood. It simply means that the person is able to make good decisions regarding their actions when they are faced with a difficult situation. They have the ability to process their emotions in order to make decisions that aren't fueled by their feelings alone.

*L*ow emotional intelligence plays a significant role in the way we interact with other people. People with low emotional intelligence often make social situations and interactions with other people tense and difficult. You can see how this would lead to difficulty analyzing people. Individuals with low EI tend to be very oblivious regarding other people's emotions and feelings. For instance, they have a hard time under-standing why their friends might be upset with them or why their co-workers are annoyed. In addition to that, they often feel like they should be the ones annoyed at other people because of other people's expectations of them to understand their feelings. While this holds true for those who have high EI, people with low EI don't have the ability to properly assess the feelings of other people. The mere topic of emotions tends to cause people with low EI to feel very exasperated as they are unable to empathize or understand why other people may feel the way they do. Due to the fact that individuals that have low EI have trouble understanding what other people's emotions are, they are often unable to feel empathy for others. They just simply do not understand what emotions the other person is feeling so it makes it very hard for them to see things from their perspective let alone empathizing.

Further, people that have low EI tend to feel that they are always right and will intensely defend their stance and refuse to hear what other people may have to say. These people tend to be pessimists and are very critical of other people's feelings.

Below we will look at a list of common attributes of people with a low level of emotional intelligence.

- Find themselves getting into arguments with others often
- Have great difficulty understanding other people's feelings and emotions
- Feel that other people should be less sensitive
- Do not find value in listening to the perspectives or feelings of other people and therefore they do not pay attention to the perspectives of others.

- Blame other people when things do not go as planned or when problems arise
- Have difficulty handling situations that involve emotions and feelings
- They have trouble regulating their emotions and this often leads to sudden outbursts of emotions
- Find it difficult to maintain friendships with people as their low level of EI ultimately gets in the way
- Have trouble understanding the feelings of others and therefore lack empathy

*T*here has been quite a lot of talk about empathy in this chapter so far, and before we go any further, I want to take some time to delve into the term deeper, as it is something that will come up over and over throughout this book.

*E*mpathy is the ability to share someone else's feelings. It is also the ability to understand the feelings of another. It also involves responding according to this shared emotion. There are different types of empathy that can exist as well. The most common type and that which I have just defined is called *Affective Empathy*. The next type of empathy is called *somatic empathy*. This type of empathy involves a real, physical reaction to someone else's feelings. For example, if you see that your friend is embarrassed, and your face starts to turn red out of second-hand embarrassment. The third and final type of empathy is cognitive empathy. This type of empathy is when you are able to understand another person's feelings to the point of being able to understand their mental state when feeling that emotion and being able to imagine what they may be thinking or what their thought process may be.

. . .

*T*he difference between empathy and sympathy is that sympathy only involves feeling sorry for the feelings someone else is going through, whereas empathy involves putting yourself in their shoes in order to feel what they must be feeling.

*H*ow To Improve Your Level Of Emotional Intelligence

You now know the value of a high level of emotional intelligence, and here we will look at what you can do to take matters into your own hands and improve your level of emotional intelligence over time. Below are several different things that you can put into practice in order to increase your emotional intelligence and thus, your ability to analyze other people.

- Reflect on yourself and your emotions

*W*hen a person reflects on their emotions, they begin to gain self-awareness. In order to grow emotional intelligence, start off by thinking about your own feelings and how you react to negative situations. When you become more aware of which emotions you are dealing with, you can begin to manage and control them appropriately.

- Listen to and accept other perspectives

*E*veryone's perception of reality is different. Start by asking others for their opinion and try to understand what you are like during emotionally charged situations.

- Observe and listen

*O*nce you have started being more self-aware, try to get a better understanding of your behavior. Begin to observe your emotions and pay attention to them.

- Pause for a moment

*S*top to think about what emotions you are feeling before you act. It may be difficult to do this in emotionally heated situations but with practice it will become a habit.

- Work on your level of empathy

*Y*ou can build more empathy by understanding the 'why' behind somebody's emotions or feelings. Try to step into their shoes and imagine how it would feel to be them.

- Take criticism gracefully

*O*bviously, nobody likes criticism, but it is an inevitable part of life. Decide to learn from criticism rather than jumping into defense mode, this way you can improve your emotional intelligence.

- Work on yourself and practice it

*I*mproving emotional intelligence does not happen overnight, however, it is something that is proven to improve with some practice.

*H*ow Is It Useful In Helping You Analyze People?

By developing a high level of emotional intelligence, you will find that it helps you to analyze people much better. For example, with a higher level of emotional intelligence, you are able to do the following with ease,

1. Show resilience even if you don't agree with another person, allowing you to listen effectively and understand their thoughts and feelings.
2. Show flexibility, which allows you to put yourself aside in order to understand the people that you are trying to analyze.
3. You will be able to listen actively, which is highly effective in analyzing people because the better you can listen, the more you can understand another person.
4. You will be able to understand other people's problems and show compassion to them.
5. You will be effective when navigating complex and difficult situations, allowing you to remain calm and understand other people's responses to situations, which is quite telling when trying to analyze them.
6. Show an excellent emotional response to other people's thoughts and feelings, making them feel comfortable enough to open up to you and share their deeper thoughts and feelings, helping you to analyze them on a deeper level.

*W*hen it comes to the ability to understand your own emotions and the emotions of other people, high emotional intelligence is required. Naturally, a person that has high emotional intelligence are better at communication as they have a good grasp on how others are feeling and how they can properly express their emotions. By being able to better understand the emotions and actions of yourself, this will help you to better understand the emotions and actions of others, which is essential in being able to analyze people.

*E*motional intelligence has grown in importance over the years, especially when it comes to the workplace. Just because you walk into your workplace it does not mean that all your emotions that you were feeling that day gets automatically put away. Although it often appears that way to most people, in reality, emotions are always existent in the workplace but they are normally kept in check in order to remain professional. People often pretend that they do not have emotions during work hours to avoid appearing unprofessional.

*I*n society today, emotional intelligence is very important because of how workplace culture is different. Nowadays, most work is done in teams and not as individuals. Employers that are forward-thinking are realizing that acknowledging emotions in the workplace tend to build better working environments. This would mean that people have to be more aware and conscious of other people's feelings along with their own. People who have better emotional intelligence are more adaptable to change which is a required skill in today's fast paced environment.

*L*eaders in the workplace that have higher emotional intelligence tend to have happier employees which lower major costs like attrition and increases overall workplace productivity. Like we discussed earlier, people who have higher emotional intelligence tend to live a happier life outside of the workplace due to lower risk of disorders like depression and anxiety.

*U*nderstanding this is not only beneficial to you if you are in a leadership position, but also if you are an employee whom this kind of environment affects directly. By being able to analyze people and show them how you are feeling, this can help you to improve your workplace environment and keep yourself, your employees and your coworkers happy.

HOW TO TELL IF YOU ARE BEING LIED TO

No matter how much a person may want to conceal the fact that they are telling a lie, there are tell-tale signs to look for that even the best liars have a hard time concealing, as they often happen without the person's control. The body naturally acts in a different and specific way when we are saying something that we do not truly believe. we have virtually no control over these subconscious actions. There are many ways to determine when someone is telling you a lie, and we will look at these ways in depth in this chapter.

Why Is This Important?

As you begin practicing using this information and the techniques which you will learn in this chapter, you will become better and better at spotting a lie in its early stages. You will become better at recognizing people who have lied to you in the past and can look for signs of compulsive liars in your life. As you become an expert, people will know that they cannot get their lies past you and they will avoid trying to convince you of things that are untrue. On the other hand, you may want to keep these skills to yourself and keep the knowledge that someone is lying to you to yourself, in order to analyze them further and further as they weave their tales.

*I*n addition to this, we now live in a time where we are bombarded with different forms of media every hour of the day, it has become important to be able to sort through it in order to pick out the important pieces of information. Being able to discern when you are being told the truth and when you are being presented falsehood is absolutely necessary. The media will tend to place emphasis on the things that they would like society to focus on, and it is an important skill to be able to determine how much of it will affect your life. In analyzing the media as well as in your own interactions, picking out falsehoods can save you from wasting much of your already limited time. If we are unable to detect a lie, we may spend years with a person we barely know, we may spend dollars on beauty techniques that have over-promised, we may invest time in friends who do not have our best interests at heart. The skills learned throughout this book are much more far-reaching than you may have imagined. These skills and techniques can be taken with you into every minute of your life from here forward.

*W*hat To Look Out For

In this section, we are going to look at the specific areas of the body that you should look to in order to find out if you are being told a lie. We will begin with the eyes, as they are very telling in this type of scenario. There are also many verbal cues to look for when a person is lying that we will look at in this section too.

1. THE EYES

The first body part we will look to is the eyes. The eyes can be very telling when trying to decipher truth from a lie. People tend to shift their gaze and avoid eye contact when they are telling a lie. This is because the eyes are a very telling part of the body and this is a well-known fact. People will avoid eye contact because they fear that if they allow you to look into their eyes, they will be given away instantly. Some others will make too much eye contact, looking you in the eyes so intently as if to study your reaction and determine if you are believing them or not. Watch for unusual amounts of eye contact, especially compared to their normal. If they are usually a person that is uncomfortable with eye contact, but they are looking you straight in the eyes, or vice versa, chances are they are trying to hide something from you. The person may also shift their eyes in all different directions, searching for ways to seem more convincing. Another thing that people may do with their eyes is to close them when telling a lie. This has two benefits for them; it shields their eyes from you, and it shields them from your reaction.

2. BODY LANGUAGE

This person may be fidgeting with their hands or their body in general because they are feeling uncomfortable. Not seeming relaxed in their body language is a telltale sign. It is very hard to feel relaxed when trying to get away with a lie and this shows in many different ways. The person may be moving their feet quite a bit, fidgeting with an inanimate object or their hair and will probably be unable to sit still or even prefer to stand. They may begin pacing or picking things up to occupy their nervous hands.

*T*he person lying will demonstrate unconfident body language. This involves closing in on oneself by crossing their arms over their chest and lowering their head and their shoulders and hunching forward. This is a posture that indicates someone is trying to make themselves small and unnoticeable. This posture could be a subconscious action simply because they feel like they would like to disappear or leave the situation. They may seem as if they would rather be anywhere else in the world than in front of you having the current conversation. This can show in the direction of their feet or by their subtle movements towards an exit.

*T*he person may be trying to cover up any signs of lying showing in their body language by trying to act extremely relaxed and calm. If the persons seem to be calm to the point where the level of relaxation is inappropriate for the situation, this could be a sign of a lie. For example, when someone commits a crime and is being questioned for it as a suspect. Naturally, they are afraid of being caught and they know that this may show. To avoid being exposed by their own fear they will feign calmness to the point where they are the calmest person in the room, slouching in their chair and playing games on their smartphone. This gives them away as anybody would be at least a little bit scared in this situation. They may also act quite jumpy and on-edge. While these two ways of acting seem opposite each other, the type of action they choose will vary depending on the gravity of the lie they are telling. They may be shifting their head from side to side almost glancing to see if anybody is around to catch them, or frantically scanning the people they are speaking to in order to see if they are believing what is being said.

3. BIOLOGICAL CHANGES

People's breathing may change when they are lying. Breathing is a process that goes on mostly without our conscious intervention. When we are nervous, our breathing changes on its own as a response to the brain thinking that there is some type of threat present. This can be a sign to look for when detecting a liar. If they are lying to you and they are feeling nervous about it they will not be able to control how their body changes their breathing. Look for changes in breathing as a quick and mostly fool-proof sign.

As mentioned in the first chapter of this book, our emotions will often cause physiological changes that we cannot control. These changes include automatic sweating, dilated pupils, tearing up or crying when sad and shaking when afraid. If a person is lying and is trying to emulate any of these emotions, we can look for signs of automatic bodily responses that accompany the emotion. If a person is lying by saying that they are feeling distraught about something, we can examine their eyes to see if they are tearing up at all. Some people are able to create tears on command, but their eyes and face will look very different from that of someone who is uncontrollably crying because of their strong feelings of sadness. When analyzing a person to detect a lie, be aware not to mistake the signs of fear for truthful feelings. We must be careful to determine whether their shaking hands and dilated pupils are being caused by their fear about the even that has occurred, or if it is because of their fear of being caught for it. Their fear could also be caused by the fear of lying. This can become complicated so we must use these bodily signs of fear in conjunction with other signs

180

of a lie in order to accurately decode the person's nonverbal communication.

4. THE HANDS

The other are the hands. People tend to subconsciously bring their hands up around their face when lying because they are automatically trying to cover the signs of lying that will inevitably show on different areas of their face. They may be trying to cover their mouth, as it is a commonplace that shows emotion, they may cover their eyes with their hands in an effort to shield themselves from your reaction if they feel that you are not buying their lie, or to hide the movements of their eyes or the fact that they will make an unusual amount of eye contact- either too much or too little.

5. THE FACE

This brings us to face twitches or micro expressions as they are called. These are the small, subconscious and virtually uncontrollable facial expressions that occur when we feel intense bursts of emotion. We discussed these in chapter 2. These will occur and show a person's true emotions that they are trying to hide. Since the face has so many small muscles, it is virtually impossible to control what goes on, especially when it comes to intense emotion. It is even more difficult to try to control our face when we are also trying to control the rest of our body and its language to cover up a lie. In some instances, people will say they feel one way when their face will show another. An example of this is a criminal trying to cover up a lie they told to a detective investigating the case. If the criminal thinks that the detective is believing their lies, their face will briefly show a happy expression (as discussed in chapter two). These micro-expressions can be used to solve crimes and is one of the reasons that questioning sessions like these are recorded for playback at a later time. The video can be slowed, and these quick twitches of emotional expression can be better detected. Much research can be done on these videos after people are found to be guilty so that more information can be gathered on lying and what this looks like on the body. Another way these facial expressions can be useful to us is their timing. These natural expressions normally occur and fade very quickly, especially since they are out of our control. If someone is faking an emotion, the accompanying facial expression they would consciously make will happen at a much more delayed rate than the natural expression would. You may even see that their initial quick expression is different from the one that they make afterward. This is an indication that they are feeling the way that their face looked initially but then they chose to put on another, different expression to convince you that this is how they feel.

6. The Voice and Verbal Cues

The person will likely change their tone of voice and the speed at which they are speaking. They may speak very quickly, much more quickly than normal. They would do this in an attempt to speed past places of incongruence or potential holes in the story. They may also do this at parts where they think you might attempt to ask questions or for clarification. They may also speak very slowly for certain parts of their story. They would do this at a place in the story that they need you to believe in order for them to get away with their lie. They may be giving their words time to sink in by emphasizing them and speaking them slowly. Another reason why they may speak very slowly is to give themselves time to come up with a lie on the spot. They may not have thought it through completely and may need some time to come up with it and because of this, buy themselves time by slowing down their words.

Further, they may stutter or get tripped up by their words as they try to concoct a lie.

*T*here are also verbal signs to look for when determining a lie. The first clue that someone is telling you a lie is that they begin to talk about themselves less and tell the story in terms of the others involved. They will put distance between them and the story or situation in an attempt to feel more comfortable with telling the story. They do this also in an attempt to make themselves feel better morally by telling the story as if they are not included. Another verbal clue is that the person may go into much more detail than is normal. Sometimes in an attempt to make their story seem as believable as possible, a person will begin adding too many details in order to make it seem like they were really there. In reality, most often we cannot remember every detail of a situation we present for and we only remember the basic sequence of events and a few details mostly relating to ourselves. The chances of remembering details about every little aspect of the situation are very slim and if a person claims to, they are most likely creating the story in the mind. As you can probably imagine, they may also begin to contradict themselves or tell the story in a different order than they did previously. They may have a hard time remembering an entire made-up days' worth of events after the initial telling.

*T*elling A White Lie Versus Telling A Big Lie

Can we tell when someone is telling us a small, or a 'white lie' to the same degree as we can tell if someone is telling us a big and very serious lie? The answer proves to be in the hands of the person telling the lie. The degree to which they believe what they are saying will determine how much this lie shows through in their body language. If the person is telling a small lie, it is much easier for them to convince themselves that they believe what they are saying. Such as your partner telling you that they called the mortgage broker last week when they actually didn't call until yesterday. They may easily convince themselves that this lie is necessary and that it is 'basically the same thing'. Because of this, their brain will not be at great odds with their words. They will not feel the need to ensure they are covering up their lie at all costs. On the other hand, if the person is telling a big lie that has major life consequences, chances are that they have thought about their lie quite a bit and their brain is fully aware of what really happened. They will have a difficult time convincing their brain that this is not a lie and that they believe the words that are coming out of their mouth. This is the case where their eyes or facial expressions will deceive them. Detecting a small lie may be more difficult but will depend on the person and what they consider to be moral and wrong.

IDENTIFYING PERSONALITY TYPES

IN THIS CHAPTER, we will be taking a look at the 16 personality types and how each of them tends to act and behave, which will help you to identify them during your analysis of people. By understanding the different personality types, you will be able to understand people on a much deeper level by understanding what makes them tick and how they would react in any given situation.

*a*n Introduction To Personality Types

The term personality is a way of describing one's potential behaviors and actions in any given situation. This means that determining someone's personality and even your own can give you insight into how and why you or another person may act. It is, in a way a description of your character as it examines and explains your thoughts, behaviors, and feelings.

· · ·

*T*here are four different categories we look at when determining personality types. Each category has two different options to choose from. People will tend to fit into one of the two options. These four categories come together in a unique combination for the person, to create many different personality types. We will examine each of the four categories in depth before learning how they come together to create personality types.

*T*he first category we will examine is introvert and extrovert, the second is sensing and intuition, next is thinking and feeling and finally judging and perceiving. Each of these traits is given a letter that represents it for ease of giving each of the different combinations a name. As you can imagine, the letters for each trait are as follows; introvert (I), extrovert (E), sensing (S), intuition (N), thinking (T), feeling (F), judging (J) and finally, perceiving (P). You may see the different personality types referred to by their corresponding letters in the future, but you can simply reference this section as a guide.

*I*ntrovert vs. Extrovert

*K*nowing whether someone is an introvert or an extrovert is a way of understanding the type of interactions they tend to prefer. Extroverts are types of people who gain energy from being around others, who enjoy crowds and many people and who become excited and energized by this. Introverts, on the other hand, are the types of people who become energized by spending more time by themselves, or who may need time after extended interaction to regain energy from within. They do not enjoy large groups or being constantly surrounded by others as much as extroverts do. While you may be thinking that you are a bit of both of these, most people can see a little of each in themselves, but whichever one we lean more towards the majority of the time is the one which you will classify yourself or someone else by. Whether someone is an introvert or an extrovert can be determined from the outside as an observer by seeing if the person seems to thrive in groups or with others, or if they seem to retreat and prefer time in a quieter environment. Think of yourself over a day and which source you draw your energy from- others or within yourself. Knowing this about yourself will help you to know what you are looking for in others.

Sensing vs. Intuition

The next category that is included in determining personality types is sensing (or observing) and intuition. This category looks at how we process the world and how we see it. People who tend to be sensing or observing variety prefer practicality and routine. They place emphasis on the past and use it to make decisions. Individuals who are the intuitive variety use their creativity to imagine possibilities and make decisions in this way. they prefer newness over routine and are very curious. In general, this could be seen in a similar manner to the left-brain, right-brain theory, where people are said to be either more left or right-brain dominant. The right brain is more creative and imaginative while the left brain is more reasonable and calculative.

. . .

*T*hinking vs. Feeling

The third category we will delve into is thinking and feeling. A pretty straight-forward category, this particular one looks at how we decide things in our life and how we handle our emotions. People who are more thinking individuals make decisions based on rationality and prefer to take an objective stance on things. They prefer to make decisions by thinking them through using their knowledge and their thoughts. These are the type of people who would make a list of pros and cons before making a decision. They tend to keep their emotions inside and do not readily express them or take them into account. On the other hand, feeling individuals are much more in touch with what they are feeling. Their emotions play a large part in their decision making. They tend to be more sensitive and express their emotions more readily than thinking individuals. They embrace their emotions and use them as a tool rather than a hindrance.

*J*udging vs. Perceiving

The fourth and final category that contributes to determining personality types is Judging and Perceiving. This section of personality is concerned with how we view and tackle work and making plans. Individuals who are of the judging variety tend to be organized and lead a well-thought-out life. They are comfortable with closure and planning in advance. While perceiving individuals lean towards a life filled with spontaneity and flexibility. They enjoy seeing what will happen and planning as they go. They are open to looking for new opportunities and are more comfortable changing plans on a whim.

. . .

*E*ach person will fall into one of the two sides of each category. This means that there are many different combinations that can come out of this type of personality examination.

Everyone will have a four-letter personality type, and this will come with some examples of the types of people that you will encounter. For our purposes, we need to understand that these 4 letters signify four different specifics about personality. Through this, we can examine people from the perspective of each of these categories on their own, or the personality type as a whole. Seeing someone become very anxious because of unmade plans can signal that they are the judging type of personality. Seeing someone that is very closed off and maybe even cold when making decisions could tell us that they are a thinking type of personality. And the same person doing both of these at once can tell us that they are the judging, thinking type of person. Being able to read this in a person will give insight into how they may react if you were to hire them for a job or a position that requires a lot of spontaneity and adapting to last-minute changes and may tell you that this person would not be a great fit for the role. There are many ways that understanding personality will be a benefit when analyzing people in your real life.

*T*hese personality types are displayed in 4-letter combinations such as ENFJ: Extrovert, Intuitive, Feeling, Judging. The four categories and the personality traits they represent all interact with one another to create a dynamic person. Everyone displays one of these combinations that can be seen when examining people's actions and body language.

. . .

What This Tells You About A Person

As discussed, these 4 options come together uniquely for each person in order to create combinations that are the different personality types. These personalities manifest themselves in displays of body language. With this understanding, we can get a sense of someone's personality type by examining their body language and what it is telling us. For example, if someone is an extrovert their body language will look very different than someone who is an introvert. And someone who is a thinking introvert will communicate with their body in a very different way than someone who is a feeling extrovert. By understanding how to read personality types through body language we can determine a lot more about a person than by simply talking to them.

How To Read And Analyze Them

Below you will see the different personality types and what they tell you about a person and how they will act. Each of these personality types are slightly different and being familiar with all of them will help you in analyzing people.

STJ – The Inspector

TSJs seem to be intimidating at first glance. These are people that appear to be proper, formal and serious. They love upholding traditional old-school values that celebrates cultural responsibility, honor, hard work and patience. These people appear to be reserved, quiet, and calm. ISTJs are wise, logical and bright individuals who have a very direct communication style. They love facts and they tend to have a lot of information that they memorize in their mind. Here are some of the main traits that an ISTJ has:

- Organized and traditional: They place high value on traditional systems and ways of doing things.
- Confident: They are confident in themselves and know exactly what types of people that they like to spend time with.
- Strong sense of duty: They are naturally not in tune with their own emotions, they often struggle with keeping up with their own and other people's emotional needs. However, they are very supporting and caring to people that they love.
- Extremely faithful: They value security and peace. They will have a mindset that is family-oriented and traditional.

*I*NFJ – The Counselor

*I*NFJs are idealists and visionaries who are full of creativity and amazing ideas. They have a unique and profound way of seeing the world and they have depth in the way they think. They don't take anything at surface level and don't just accept things for the way they are. Some people may see INFJs as weird due to their unique view on life. These people are highly intuitive, complex, caring and gentle. They are creative and artistic and live in a world that is full of possibilities and hidden meanings for them to decipher. One of their main qualities is their mysteriousness. INFJs can be people that are tough to understand from the outside but are very caring and warm to their loved ones. Here are some of the main traits of an INFJ:

- Secretive: They appear to be reserved and quiet and often stay away from social situations where they have to mingle with people that they don't know. It takes them some time to build trust with people.
- Sensitive: They are sensitive towards the feelings of other people and place a lot of care in trying not to hurt people through their actions and words.
- Strategist and planner: Their creativity makes them stand out to people.
- Firm: They have firm and stubborn traits and they don't tend to stray away from their values. They have a temper when other people question their principles and beliefs.

INTJ – The Mastermind

People with the INTJ personality type is often known as 'the mastermind'. These people are introverts, reserved and quiet. They are self-sufficient people that would prefer to work individually than with others. They find that socializing drains their energy as they are introverted so they feel the need to recharge after a lot of social exposure. INTJs are interested in theories and ideas. They observe the world in a way where they are always questioning why things are the way they are. They are excellent at developing strategies and plans and don't like the unknown. INTJs firmly believe that they are a capable and intelligent person. Their versatile minds causes them to enjoy intellectual challenges and they may feel bored when their intellect isn't stimulated. Here are some of the main traits of the INTJ:

- Ambitious: They are self-confident, ambitious and deliberate people. They are committed to always finding the best strategy to express their ideas.
- Ruthless: They are ruthless when it comes to analyzing effectiveness of ideas or methods. This trait makes them efficient decision-makers, often beginning at a young age.
- Difficulties: They struggle with dealing with things that do not require logical reasoning. This weakness that they have is prominent within their interpersonal relationships. They struggle to handle romantic relationships.

 NFJ – The Giver

ENFJ's are people-focused. They are ethical, highly principled, outspoken, charismatic, idealistic and extroverted. They understand how to connect with people regardless of their personality and background. ENFJs tend to live within their imagination and not the real world. Rather than focusing on the 'here and now', ENFJs concentrate on what could happen in the future and the abstract of it all. These people tend to be influential even if they're not trying. Their confidence and influence comes from their altruism and authenticity. They are reliable, loyal and genuinely kind for no other reason than simply just wanting the best for themselves and the people around them. Here are some of their main traits:

- Charisma: They tend to fight for the 'true' meaning of life and to find the purpose in the bigger picture. Many ENFJs become social workers, humanitarians and politicians.
- Strive to find balance: They find pleasure when they are in the company of others but they also strive to have alone time. They tend to try to find the balance between these two extremities.

ISTP – The Craftsman

ISTPs are people that are mysterious, logical and rational. At the same time they are quite enthusiastic and spontaneous. Their personality traits are not as recognizable than some of the bolder personality types and even the people that they know closely struggle to anticipate their reactions and behaviors. However, ISTPs are spontaneous deep down and are unpredictable, they try to hide these traits from others. ISTPs are generous and optimistic and believe that equality and fairness are important things in the world. They have a strong drive to find an understanding of how all things work and are good at logical analysis. Here are some of their main traits:

- Unable to stay focused: They tend to live in the present

and love new experiences, however their spontaneous-ness makes it hard for them to stay focused on one task.

- Fairness and equality: They make their decisions from a sense or practical realism. They make sure that their decisions reflect equality and fairness. They are loyal to their loved ones but they require a lot of time to recharge by being alone.

ESFJ – The Provider

ESFJs are your stereotypical extroverts. These people are the social butterflies and have a need to interact and make other people happy. This usually makes them very popular. In movies, the ESFJ is likely the cheerleader in college or high school. They continue to have their spotlight later on in life and is the person that is focused on organizing social gatherings for their loved ones. ESFJ is one of the most common personality types and is one that is liked by nearly everyone. These people are the life of the party, while they enjoy being the center of attention, they also like listening to the things that other people have to say. They like conversation that is more than just small talk, they like to hear about their loved one's activities and relationships. They will remember small details of conversations and are always ready to listen to others with genuine warmth. Here are some of the common traits of ESFJs:

- Trap: These people are true altruists and are always trying to do the right thing. However, the right thing is normally based on their traditions. They base what is true not on philosophical theories but based on what authority says.

- Role models: An ESFJs love for socialization and people will place them naturally in a position of power. They thrive in leadership roles as long as their efforts are appreciated by people who care.

I NFP – The Idealist

I NFPs are introverts, and like most of them they are reserved and quiet. They prefer to not talk about themselves especially when they are first meeting someone new. They enjoy spending their time alone in quiet places so they can analyze the things that are happening around them. INFPs love analyzing symbols and signs and think of them as metaphors that have a deeper meaning in life. They often get lost in their daydreams and imaginations and drown themselves in their thoughts, ideas and fantasies. INFPs main goals are to discover the true meaning of life and to help humanity. They are both perfectionists and idealists who motivate themselves to achieve goals. They are very intuitive about people and rely on their own intuitions to make it through life. In conflict situations, INDPs will try to understand both sides of an argument and will avoid hurting anybody's feelings at all costs.

- Gut feelings: Other people may make their decisions based on past experiences, INFPs rely on their gut feelings and their intuition.
- Talented: They are often talented writers. Although they

are uncomfortable with expressing themselves verbally, they have a strong ability to express their feelings on paper.

*E*SFP – The Performer

*E*SFPs are people that are observant, extroverted, and observant. They are often seen as 'the entertainers'. These people are naturals in front of other people and capture the attention of an audience, they also love the spotlight. ESFPs are explorers who love to learn and then share what they've learnt with other people. They have strong interpersonal skills and love to be in the center of attention. They are friendly, generous, sympathetic, warm and genuinely concerned for other people's wellbeing. Although from the outside it doesn't seem this way, ESFPs know that not everything is about them. They are empathetic to their loved ones. They also rely more on luck rather than opportunity. They will simply just as for help when they need it. Here are some of the main traits of the ESFP:

- Show-off: They are known to be people that are talkative, highly social, outgoing and a bit of a show-off. They enjoy being the center of attention and performing for others.
- Strong sense of adventure: They enjoy spending time with other people and getting to know others. They even have a knack for making others happy. They have a desire to learn and explore new things.
- Neglect: Their primary focus is on immediate gratifications and pleasure, oftentimes this is so much that they tend to

neglect their responsibilities in order to enjoy their pleasures for longer.

- Face value: They are likable people who find happiness in the smallest moments in life. They have an honest approach to most aspects in life and try to take everything at face value.

*E*NFP – The Champion

*E*NFPs have perceiving, feeling, intuitive and extraverted personality. They are very individualistic and strive to create their own ideas, actions, methods, looks and habits. They don't like people who are cookie cutter and hate when they aren't able to think outside the box. They like to be around others who also have a strong intuitive nature. ENFPs tend to be good at many things and can usually achieve success in anything that is of interest to them. However, they do get bored very easily and are not good at following activities through until it's completed. They should avoid jobs that require a lot of routine tasks. Here are some of the main traits of an ENFP:

- Manipulative: They need lots of time alone in order to make sure they are moving in a direction that matches their values. ENFPs have a lot of charm and they can get quiet manipulative since their charisma allows them to get what they want easily.
- Lavishing love: Relationships are an important part to their lives so they tend to be very involved with their romantic relationships. They have a tendency to fish for

compliments and likes to hear affirmations from their loved ones that they are valued.

- Difficult time disciplining: Their affection and enthusiasm may seem as if they are smothering to their own children. Routine things like picking up their kids from day care can seem like a huge chore and is not in their natural strength. They have a tough time disciplining their children.

- Good at most things: They are enthusiastic and warm people who have a lot of potential. They tend to have a broad range of skills and are good at almost everything that interests them.

 STP – The Doer

ESTPS are people that have perceptive, thinking, sensing and extraverted personalities. They need social interaction, logical processes and reasoning, feelings and emotions, and a huge need for freedom. Abstracts and theories don't keep the attention for an ESTP and most people with this personality type tend to make decisions before they have thought about it clearly and will fix their mistakes as they arise. ESTPs spontaneous ways of life makes certain school and work environments challenging for them to navigate through. This is not due to the fact that they aren't hard working or unintelligent, simply it's because they don't believe in regulated and structured environments. Here are some of the main traits of an ESTP:

- Full of passion: They like to keep things interesting while growing themselves without needing to disrupt normal society.

- Work hard play hard: They are spontaneous and spirited people, they often are go-getters who like to be engaged and active. Making new friends and networking with people come very naturally.
- Unpredictability: They don't spend much time planning their life or their future, but their enthusiasm and desire for unpredictability make them people that are entertaining and spontaneous.

$\mathcal{E}$STJ – The Supervisor

$\mathcal{E}$STJs are organized, traditional, honest, dedicated and believers of the fact that what their doing is socially responsible and right. They make themselves the leader of the pack who navigate through the path of 'good' and 'right'. They are the definition of good citizens. People tend to look up to ESTJs for counsel and guidance. They are always happy when they are approached for help. They thoroughly enjoy being role models and helping out with events in their community in order to bring people together. Here are some of the main traits of an ESTJ:

- Extremely organized: These people are very firm on following the law and does not believe in laziness. They have the strong ability to make the hardest tasks seem simply and easy.
- Judgmental: They are extroverts and enjoy working alongside with other people. This makes them feel angry if

other people around them are dishonest, unreliable and lazy.

- Hardworking: They have a hard time dealing with the fact that other people have different views and they struggle to understand that others may not want to follow the same life trajectory as they do. However, their hardworking character enables them to play a leadership role that works with most people.

$\mathcal{E}$ NTJ – The Commander

$\mathcal{A}$ n ENTJs main mode of living entirely focuses on dealing with all external aspects as logically and rationally as possible. They are natural born leaders which like to be in charge. They live in a world where they see challenges simply as obstacles that are an opportunity for them to push themselves. They have a natural leadership gift and are great at making decisions while considering all angles of a problem quickly and carefully. ENTJs enjoy to be with people but find it hard to get really close to people. They struggle to see things outside from their own perspective. Here are some of the main traits of an ENTJ:

- Forceful: They tend to be overbearing, forceful, and intimidating which are traits they have to overcome when at school, work or family.
- No limit: They enjoy a good challenge regardless if it's big or small. They believe that there isn't a limit to what they can achieve as long as they are given enough time and resources to achieve them. They often don't care about

how others view them and place more importance on accomplishing their goals.

- Growth-oriented: They have an approach and outlook on life and relationships that are growth-oriented and they will jump on any opportunity in order to improve themselves.

INTP – The Thinker

INTPs are well known for their unrelenting logic and brilliant theories. They are arguably the most logical out of all 16 personality types. They have a great eye for finding discrepancies and love following patterns. They also are strong in reading people which makes it a bad idea to try to deceive them. INTPs are not interested in the practical day to day activities but they excel in environments where they can express their potential and reactivity. INTPs are original, unconventional, and independent. They do not hold much value in goals like security and popularity, rather they have a complex character and tend to be more temperamental and restless. They are ingenious and have thought patterns that are not conventional which allows them to analyze things in new ways. Here are the main traits of an INTP:

- Scientific breakthroughs: They see everything in a light of how it can be improved or transformed into. INTPs are at their best when they can independently work on their theories.
- Live within their own head: INTPs seem to be distant to other people because of how often they spend their time

inside their own minds. They are driven to transform problems into explanations that are logical which makes them spend so much of their time living in their own heads.

- Extremely bright: They value knowledge above everything else and they approach problems with skepticism and enthusiasm. They are bright in the way that they have the ability to be objectively critical in their analysis.
- Tolerant: They do not like to be in a leadership role as they are people that are very flexible and tolerant in most situations.
- Not in-tune: They hold little value for decisions that are made due to their feelings. They strive to find logical conclusions to every problem. Due to this, they are not in-tune to the feeling of others and their emotional needs.

*I*SFJ – The Nurturer

*I*SFJs are philanthropists that are ready to give back to the work with generosity. They believe that the world is upheld by enthusiasm and unselfishness. ISFJs are people that are kind-hearted and warm. They heavily value cooperation and harmony and are very sensitive to the feelings of other people. People often value ISFJs for their awareness, consideration and their ability to bring out the best parts of other people. ISFJs are naturally hard workers and are very meticulous to the point where it is nearing perfectionism. They have a personal interest in their work and often try to go above and beyond with everything they do. Not only do they want to meet expectations, they want to exceed all expectations. Here are some of the main traits of an ISFJ:

- Startlingly accurate: They constantly are storing and taking in information about people and situations. They are able to store a tremendous amount of information that is accurate due to their exceptional memory.
- Strive to attain: ISFJs value kindness and security and respects laws and traditions. They believe that current existing systems are there for a reason and they likely will not do anything in a new and innovative way.
- Powerful emotions: ISFJs do not normally express their feelings unless they find the right outlet for their strong emotions. They are dependable, generous and warm and often have many special gifts to offer.

*E*NTP – The Visionary

*E*NTPs are one of the rarest personality types in the world. They are extroverts but they also do not enjoy small talk and don't thrive in most social situations. ENTPs are people that are knowledgeable and intelligent, but they have the need to be always mentally stimulated. They have a strong ability to discuss facts and theories in extensive detail. These people are objective, rational and logical in their approach to arguments and information. ENTPs get great pleasure from participating in discussions that are intellectual, such as debates. They are unafraid to question many things and will dismiss other people's ideas or thoughts if they cannot find logical justification. Here are some of the main traits of an ENTP:

- Detached: ENTPs are people that are humorous, but they can also come off as condescending and arrogant. They can be very sociable people, but they can also be very detached from others.
- Visionary: ENTPs are very intuitive, they have an ability to find patterns and trends while still looking at the big picture. Their personality allows them to create big and eccentric ideas that may be the key to solutions that the world needs.
- Freedom-loving: ENTPS are people that love freedom. They don't like to control others, nor do they want to be controlled. They create new opportunities and are also receptive to them, but they will not be tied down to standards and rules.
- Direct: ENTPs may not be the most likeable people although they try to be as friendly as possible. They don't seek approval from others and they often prefer to work alone and have a bit of a superiority complex.

$\mathcal{I}$ SFP – The Composer

$\mathcal{I}$ SFPs are introverts that do not come off as one. They often have difficulty building connections with people right off the bat, however, they do become friendly, approachable and warm eventually. ISFPs are fun to be around and they are spontaneous people which makes them the perfect friend to go on an adventure with. People with this personality type want to embrace the present and live their life to the fullest. They make sure to always explore new experiences and new things. They are creative, active and goal driven. They tend to make other people feel better when they are around due to their positive disposition. Here are a few of the main traits of an ISFP:

- Spontaneous: They love exploring new activities, ideas and things. They like to come up with new ideas and experiments with them.
- Artists: They have a strong passion for beauty and aesthetics. They are in tune with the way things smell, feel, sound and taste. They have a strong appreciation for art as well.
- Original and independent: They tend to hold back their opinions and ideas from most people except for a few that are hand selected. They need to have their own personal space but are independent and original.
- Care about people: ISFPs are sympathetic and warm people. They genuinely care about others and have a strong desire to please. They like to show their love through actions and not words.
- Takes life seriously: ISFPs have a strong set of values which they try to meet throughout their lives. People who don't know an ISFP may think that they are carefree and lighthearted people, however, ISFP takes their life very seriously and are constantly gathering information in search of an underlying meaning.

$\mathcal{H}$ow To Use This Knowledge To Your Advantage

Understanding personality types is important in analyzing people as this allows us to be able to account for natural differences in the way people act or display behavior simply because of what type of person they are. These personality types create different types of people who may act slightly differently in different situations. Knowing what to look for to analyze someone's personality type will aid in further analyzing their actions. This will also allow you to anticipate how they may act in different situations or respond to things you may want to say. It is an invaluable tool in analysis for understanding someone's current actions as well as their potential future reactions.

Case Studies

One thing that can influence your analysis of a person is the fact that we all enter the world each day with an idea of how we wish to be perceived. This can make analyzing a person more difficult than if they were showing their true personality in each interaction. There is more work to be done to ensure you are reading a person correctly. Luckily, growing up in a world full of people we have years of practice and informal research to use to help us. Since we all put forth some kind of image, we can understand that everyone else around us is doing this too. But knowing the common images people like to put forth can help us to weed through this in order to reach an understanding of the true person beneath it. We will examine some of the most common types of facades that you will encounter on a daily basis.

1. THE "CLASS CLOWN"

This is the 'class clown' case study. The class clown performance can be observed into adulthood, but for the purposes of understanding, this is the name we will give it. When you hear this term class clown, you likely think of the person from your school days who was always making jokes and laughing hysterically. While there are different levels of comedy a person can possess, the body language that may be observed is very similar among them. This person will stand up tall, make many gestures using their hands and arms, and often be moving around the room. They speak at loud volumes and initiate interactions the majority of the time. Is this person demonstrating their true personality, or are they looking to be accepted and adored? To determine this, we can look at the situations in which they begin to tell jokes and engage people. Do they do this immediately following constructive criticism? Do they do this immediately following a compliment being given to someone else? Do they do this as soon as they meet someone new? By examining the time and place that this person performs their comedic acts we can determine their intentions. Do they only perform in a large group, or do they use their comedy to cheer up a close friend when they are one-on-one? If the latter is the case, this person may be genuine in the demonstration of their internal traits. If the former is the case, they may be using this type of performance to gain social status. Knowing which of these is the case can help us in our analysis of this person. Discerning their motives and intentions is the first step in analyzing them. After this, we can begin to analyze changes in their body language such as volume, tone, and gestures. This will give us an even better sense of what they are truly feeling and thinking.

2. The "Lighthearted Girl"

The next type of person we will examine is what we will call the 'happy go lucky girl'. We have all known people like this in our lives. Her body language looks like the following; always smiling, wears bright colors, has many friends and is always telling stories in a very animated tone of voice. This type of girl or woman can be observed over a variety of ages and is not exclusive to a young woman. While it can be argued that this is a genuine personality type, we will examine how to break through this in order to truly see whether this is the case or not. Firstly, we can often observe this person with a big smile on their face. We know by now how to analyze whether or not this smile is genuine. We can examine their face and determine if the majority of their smiling is of a genuine nature, or if it is seemingly put on in order to please or fit in. Next, we can choose to look further than the colors and accessories they are wearing because as we know by this point, those are involved in a first impression but are not of as much importance to us in this specific analysis anymore. The animated tone of voice and carefree posture is where it becomes slightly more difficult to discern. We need to look for moments where things have gone quieter and this person is in a less performative environment. This is where we can look for clues as to what type of personality they may possess. If we are having a group conversation with them and people start to leave, does their body language change? If they are speaking in an office meeting and then the meeting ends, does their body language change? If they are in the presence of a respected person and this person leaves, does their body language change? Through the examination of scenarios like this, we may begin to see whether this person really has an extroverted, feeling personality or if they really have an introverted, thinking personality that is being overshadowed.

3. THE "BRICK WALL"

The next case study is the 'brick wall'. We all know a person who is stone cold when it comes to emotions. Have you ever heard someone refer to someone else as a tough exterior but a softie on the inside? This person appears to be very unemotional- thinking and sensing over feeling and intuition. The body language says they are ready for a challenge with their rigid posture, that they are not influenced by their emotions with their blank facial expression. Many people may take this body language at face value, but we are able to better analyze a person than that. We can observe them in times of decision making and planning. These are times when the stress of the situation can show the person's true personality. Whether in work or personal life, we can observe their true decision-making style for example. If they are choosing between two options, they may seem like they would be the type to weight out the facts of each option and come to a logical decision. Do they, however, begin discussing the emotional side of each choice, or how this is making them feel? If so, they may be putting forth the image of a brick wall, but this may not be the case at all.

4. THE PERSON WHO TAKES UP SPACE

The next personality example is the 'knee spreader'. This performance is slightly more general, but I imagine we all have a person that comes to mind when we hear this. This person is usually male, and he sits with his legs spread wide, he tends to keep his head and eyes up, he has a fairly put-together appearance and he walks with purpose. This type of person may be a business executive, an athlete, or an average man. Regardless, it can become confusing when trying to determine if his body language is a performance or if he is truly a confident and self-assured sensing personality type. We can examine this person and what types of people are in their presence when they are putting forth this type of body language. Are they around potential partners? Are they with teammates or coworkers? Do they display the same type of body language when they are with their family? On public transit? If so, then this person is likely self-assured and has a personality type that leaves them observing the world around them often. If the answer is no, however, this person may seem observant because they are examining their surroundings in order to see who is near them and how this person may come across to them if they are being their true intuitive, thinking self. Examine this type of person closely as it may be difficult to determine their true personality. The key lies in the changes in actions. When their body language changes, observe this.

YOUR OWN BODY LANGUAGE

Now that we have examined body language by the different areas of the body, we can use this information to our benefit in more ways than just analyzing people. With a deeper understanding of what body language is and the importance of it, you can begin to pay attention to your own body language and verbal communication in order to get the most out of your interactions. This goes hand in hand with your skills of analyzing people as it is a balancing act between analyzing a person and noticing your own messages through body language in order to make a person feel comfortable enough to engage in dialogue and interactions with you. In this chapter, we will look at how you can do this.

How To Convey Specific Messages With Your Own Body Language

The first situation that we will look at is how to make a person feel at ease by demonstrating that you are listening to them with the intention of understanding them, so that they continue to open up to you and share information with you. Number one below is how to show that you are listening by using specific body language. Number two, is how to show that you are a leader and in a position of power to gain respect by showing specific body language.

1. Show That you are Listening

Use body language to demonstrate that you are attentive and interested. If you seem uninterested or bored, the person is unlikely to continue sharing with you. We have probably all been in a situation where we felt we were opening up to someone and they seemed uninterested. We probably felt embarrassed or regretted being so open then. Opening up is often hard and we need to feel respected before doing so. If you want to hear what they have to say or want them to continue being open and honest with you, show this. Sit or stand with good posture- that is, shoulders back and arms open to receiving. Keep your head up and maintain eye contact, do not fidget with objects or shuffle your feet. All of these signs will show the person that you are listening to.

*S*tart by maintaining a comfortable amount of eye contact. Making eye contact for a long enough period that the other person sees this and glancing away at something every so often. Giving too much eye contact will make the person feel uncomfortable and even humiliated, as this gives the impression that you are making fun of them by over-showing the fact that you are listening to them. Next, maintain an open posture. Keep your body open to receiving this information. Keep your chest open by having your arms at your sides or comfortably resting on your legs or the table, depending on the type of environment. This shows the person that you are listening with an open mind. If you are standing, try not to lean on anything as this demonstrates boredom or tiredness. Maintain an upright but relaxed body positioning. If you are sitting, ensure that you are not resting your head in your hands as this is another indication of boredom. Sit upright in the chair, avoid slouching, and try to sit relatively still. Spinning around on the wheels of the chair will indicate that you are distracted and uninterested. Show the person that you are listening and understanding by nodding every so often and maintain a relaxed face. Smile if you feel it, but otherwise, maintain a relaxed facial expression. Too strong of a facial expression could send the message that you are in disagreement, that you find something comical or that you are frustrated by their words. This could cause them to stop talking or change their course of conversation and will have impeded your listening ability.

*S*howing someone that you are listening is much more effective than simply telling them that you are listening. They will be observing you throughout the conversation and picking up on your nonverbal communication to get a sense of what you are thinking about what they are saying. In order to listen most effectively, it is best to maintain an air of impartiality so that they will feel comfortable continuing the conversation. After you have fully listened to them, you will be better equipped to respond having understood their entire point of view.

2. Exhibit Leadership Traits

At this point, we will examine how to lead and influence using your own body language and nonverbal communication. Understanding this concept in others allows us to use it to our advantage by choosing what type of messages we wish to send. By now we know that it matters less to people what you say and more how you say it. When being a leader, it is important to know how to say things in a way that commands attention and respect and will get people listening.

*A*s humans, the traits we desire in a leader are somewhat universal. We want to feel like we can trust the person, but also that they will speak up and advocate for us when need be. We want to feel like they listen to us and understand us, while also being prepared to make decisions on our behalf that will benefit us. We want them to be the confident and self-assured face that represents us but also a relatable one. While it may seem impossible to achieve all of these different things at once, I assure you it is possible. We as humans have a difficult time deciphering real confidence from performed confidence, and we like to believe that the leaders we respect are on a pedestal while still being relatable enough that we trust them. This all comes down to showing confidence and certainty while voicing understanding and concern.

*W*hen it comes to a leader, everyone wants someone that is confident in an area where most are not. Where most feel fear and uncertainty, the leader feels confidence and security in their choices. They are not over-confident however, as this makes people fear naivety. Confidence is often underestimated as a tool for leadership. Yes, the choices a leader makes on behalf of their people is important, but the people want someone to believe in, and they will not believe in someone that does not appear to believe in themselves.

. . .

*S*o how exactly do we show our people that we are confident? This comes down to nonverbal communication. We can say as many times as we like that we are confident in what we are saying, but if our body language does not show this, we are not convincing. We are going to examine the body language of each part of a leader's body. It helps to imagine a leader you trust or imagine someone who you would want to be lead by. Get a picture in your mind's eye before reading the next paragraph. For suggestions, maybe they are someone speaking in front of an office of people, maybe a captain of a sport's team, maybe a chef in a restaurant. This leader does not have to be famous or of political status, all respected leaders share very similar body language. Now that we have this image in mind, we are going to examine it from head to toe. Confident nonverbal communication looks like the following:

*T*he number one spot we are going to discuss are the arms and hands. Because leaders often speak to large groups of people or speak to people from a distance, the arms and hands are very important. From a distance, this will be what they can see if they cannot make out the face or if they are not within earshot. A leader wants their arms and hands to demonstrate ease and comfort with what they are saying and what they stand for. If you have ever seen a leader speak in a video but you could not hear the sound, even without knowing who they are you can tell that they are a leader. This is because of their gestures and movements. Keeping your hands out and visible is a sign that you are confident and that you have nothing to hide. As humans, we tend to feed insecure if we cannot see a person's hands, especially if that person is someone leading us. Keeping your hands out and visible for all to see shows that you are being transparent and are confident in what you are standing for. While keeping your hands out, it is important to notice what they're doing. If they are fidgeting with their hair or their clothing or something on the table in front of them, they will appear nervous or anxious. If their leader appears nervous and anxious, the people will not feel secure in their leadership skills. The arms play an important role in this as well. If the arms are moving and gesturing along with what the person is saying, they appear to be enthused and passionate about what they are saying. This makes them appear to be really believing what they are saying, whereas if they are standing with their arms stiffly at their side, or if their arms are barely moving it makes them seem rehearsed and like they are not invested in their own words. Gestures that are in tune with the content of one's speech and that are not too aggressive or over the top are best. Too many gestures can also seem rehearsed and like the person is overly trying to engage people. There is a sweet spot right in the middle that feels natural and confident.

To follow the arms and hands, the next section we will examine is the stance and the feet. As mentioned earlier in chapter two, the feet are an often-forgotten piece to the puzzle of body language. The feet should be firmly planted on the ground, facing forward and not shifting nervously. While you don't want to stand like a statue, you do not want to be pacing or moving them in a way that demonstrates nerves. Leaders take up space. Both with their arm gestures and their feet. The stance is created by where the feet are placed. In a confident stance, the feet are wide enough that you are taking up space. If your feet are shoulder-width apart, this is an appropriate amount of space that is proportionate to your body size. Taking up space shows that you are secure in your position, that you are not trying to make yourself small to fit in anywhere, that you are unafraid to be seen.

. . .

*A*s with stance, posture is a demonstrator of how you feel about yourself and your position. A leader will stand with their shoulders back, their chest out and open. This is another way to take up space. Your shoulders will take up space just as your feet will, and this demonstrates confidence in yourself. Hunching your shoulders, closing up your chest space and folding yourself down is an indicator that you are trying not to be noticed, or that you are not confident. Appearing too rigid and upright can make someone seem intimidating and overly uptight, so avoid being too rigid. A nice confident but comfortable posture includes the shoulders back and the hips semi-forward.

*T*he posture of the head is important for demonstrating confidence as well. The chin should be upright, and the head should be facing forward. The head should be fairly stable when speaking or standing and even walking, as this is a natural demonstrator of confidence. Leaders avoid lowering their head or moving it from side to side as they speak as this can make them appear frantic. A leader who appears frantic is not one that people will readily trust with their best interests.

*T*he clothing a leader wears can vary greatly by culture and region, but in a general sense, the clothing choice must be of a professional nature. Professional can look like a suit, a dress, or traditional clothing, whichever is most appropriate for the setting. The choice of clothing demonstrates respect for the environment that you are in and concern for your image. Included in this are the hair and hygiene. Someone who appears to put time and effort into their clothing, their appearance, and their personal maintenance will appear to be prepared to take care of matters for their cause. If someone turns up to lead and they are unkempt and unclean, they will give off the impression that they are not able to take care of matters because they cannot take care of themselves.

*U*ntil now, we have discussed what a leader looks like from relatively far away. Body parts and actions that you would notice if you were standing at the back of the room. There are also, however, characteristics of confident body language that can be seen when closed up. Leaders must remain confident even in more intimate settings such as one-on-one discussions. We will begin with the eyes. While leading, it is important that everyone feels included and encompassed by the care of the leader. When making eye contact, slowly scan the room, attempting to make eye contact with many people rather than focusing on one or two at the front. Leaders keep their eyes up, showing attentiveness and readiness to answer a question or address a concern. They avoid choosing just one person to focus on and avoid staring at the floor or the ceiling, or at inanimate objects for too long.

*T*he way that a leader holds their face says a lot about how they are feeling. While there are those small, quick expressions that are very hard to notice or avoid, most people will not notice these. The facial expression will be noticed by people as they will be trying to get a sense of how the leader is feeling. Maintaining a neutral and relaxed facial expression will show that you are confident even in the face of a problem, that you are prepared to tackle anything. Avoid too much tension anywhere in the face and ensure that your mouth is neutral or in a light smile. Seeming mostly unphased by problems people raise will maintain their confidence in your abilities to take care of them and their concerns or problems.

*O*ne attribute of a good leader not to be forgotten is their handshake. A firm and confident handshake can be a great demonstrator of confidence. Have you ever shaken someone's hand for the first time, and it was a limp, loose handshake? This probably gave you a lot of impressions of them that you may not have otherwise had. Keeping your handshake firm and tense enough shows the person that you are secure in yourself and confident in your abilities. It is also important to make eye contact while shaking someone's hand.

*T*he next factor worth mentioning is voice-related, however, are still nonverbal forms of communication. The first is the tone of voice. Hearing someone's tone of voice is telling whether they are speaking a language you understand or not. By someone's tone of voice, we can tell what type of talking they are doing. When a leader is speaking it is best if they are speaking in a calm tone, with inflection where needed. They must sound calm and avoid sounding erratic in tone while being careful not to sound too relaxed in fear of coming across as unconcerned. Speed is another factor of voice that must be taken into account. If someone is talking with great speed, they seem nervous and rushed and this makes people feel uncomfortable. If someone is speaking too slowly, this can be insulting to the audience. The right speed is slow enough to be understood while pausing naturally where appropriate. It should feel natural enough that you can think while you are speaking. the third and final factor of voice to be addressed is volume. Someone who speaks too quietly appears unsure and tends to leave the listeners frustrated. Someone who speaks too loudly does not leave their listeners feeling engaged and can cause people to stop listening out of discomfort. Speaking at a tone where the people furthest from you can hear and understand you without blasting the front row with sound waves is the ideal volume and this demonstrates a confidence in the content of your speech as you are committed to having everyone in attendance hear what you are saying. This also avoids you having to repeat yourself which can leave you feeling nervous and flustered and will lead you to lose your air of confidence for the rest of your speech.

*B*eing a good leader also involves some degree of influence and persuasion. When it comes to the type of leadership where there is a vote that decides who the leader will be, persuasion and influence become very important as you will need to get as many people as you can to put their trust in you and select you and what you represent or stand for. Persuasion does not have to include being untruthful, as we have seen that there are many ways to identify if someone is being untruthful.

*T*here are other situations where we may want to be influential that does not involve a vote or that are not of a political nature. You may be a parent who needs to influence their child to choose something, or you may want to persuade your friend to make a certain choice. These techniques are still relevant for these types of situations as well.

*A*ppearing confident in your position is crucial when it comes to being persuasive. Just as previously discussed, appearing confident in large part depends on your nonverbal communication. If you think and act like a leader in any situation

221

you will be more convincing and believable to people, whether these people know you personally or not.

*T*he Importance Of Noticing Your Own Body Language

Self-awareness is the key to understanding oneself and in turn, understanding others. We see other people in politics, everyday life, and in the media. It is impossible to avoid being witness to all sorts of different types of body language and so opportunities are all around you. We are social creatures, and this will not change even with the introduction of so many forms of media and technology.

*B*ecause we understand what different body language actions can tell us about any given interaction, we can control what messages our own body language is sending to the other person or people we are interacting with.

*U*sing body language can show the other person or people, that you are open to listening to them and that they are being heard. As you saw above, there are very specific ways to show this. Below, I will demonstrate the importance of noticing your own body language by showing you some more specific examples of how you can reach specific personality types using different body language in order to achieve desired outcomes.

.   .   .

HOW TO ANALYZE PEOPLE

laying to someone's personality type is important in being a good listener as well as being influential. If you deem someone to be of the feeling and perceiving variety, you can use your understanding of this type of personality to communicate your position to them in the most effective way for them to understand you and why you have this stance. For someone who is a feeler and perceiver, we would approach them with the less objective and more emotional side of the issue. For example, if we are trying to influence this person to take our stance on vegetarianism being a better choice than eating meat. In this example, we would approach the conversation in an emotionally charged route, discussing the feelings of the people and animals involved, how being a vegetarian is an ethical choice, etc. For this same example, if we were dealing with someone who is a sensing and thinking individual, we would come at this persuasive effort from a different angle. We might start by explaining facts such as how much money we spend on meat each year, or how it can change our health. Using more quantitative information to persuade this type of personality would be much more effective than using their emotions as they tend to focus more on objective information than what they feel. On top of approaching the conversation differently depending on the personality type, remaining confident in body language and voice will make your position that much stronger.

n any case, where we want someone to do something, we become a leader in a way. Anyone can use these leadership techniques in their life. If you manage a group of people in your workplace you are a leader and you may want to use these techniques to appear confident in your next meeting. you also may want to use these techniques for analyzing people in the next job interview you conduct, and you may want to use these techniques for influence next time you have to deal with a difficult employee who may see a work-related matter differently than you. Body language and nonverbal communication not only benefits those who know how to read it, but also those who know how to use it to their advantage. Humans find the confidence to equal trustworthiness and this is something that will not change in the near future.

HOW TO ANALYZE PEOPLE

IN THIS SECTION, we are going to look at how you can combine everything you have learned in this book in order to analyze a person as a whole and how you can get better at this over time.

How To Put It All Together

Analyzing people is an important skill that proves to be beneficial in a wide array of situations. There is a great deal that goes into being able to accurately analyze a person. From understanding what nonverbal communication is, to knowing what type of body language to look for and what it is telling us, to using this in order to decide what body language we will use in any given situation, to leading and persuading people in a way most fitting to their specific personality. All of these things leave you well-equipped to enter the world ready to confidently take on any situation with a social advantage. The key to getting better and better at this is practice. We will look at the importance of practice and how it can help you develop this skill in the following section.

. . .

*T*he Importance Of Practice

Practice is the key to developing yourself in any way, but especially when it comes to skills of the mind. In order to become better at analyzing people, it is important to practice what you have learned in this book in real-time situations. By putting together all of the knowledge and techniques you have gained thus far, you will be able to approach any situation- professional or otherwise- as a confident and influential analyzer of people after some practice.

*I*f you are someone that is just starting out in learning how to analyze people, start easy. Start by analyzing people you already know and associating their body language, tone of voice, and verbal messages based on the mood you already know they're in. For instance, if your best friend told you that they are in a great mood, analyze what their body language is like. How does a happy person carry themselves? What are their facial expressions like? By being able to associate general cues for a happy person, you will be able to extrapolate that information to assess strangers around you.

*T*he first step in practicing these skills is to try reviewing a few case studies to see if you have picked up some knowledge from this book so far. In the next section you can put your skills to the test!

. . .

Case Studies

To give you more practice, we will look at some case studies that will help you to begin analyzing people through their displays of nonverbal communication. Try to figure out what to look for and how to read it when you see it through reading the following case studies.

Case Study #1

We will examine a case study from the animal kingdom that can also be seen in human males: the alpha male. For this guy, body language is everything. The way that they assert dominance and maintain their status as the alpha male is through their demonstration of alpha-type body language. They rely on their body language to signal to others that they are in this position and of this status. If you have ever been to the zoo, as you walk through the different sections and look at the different animals, the thing that is common amongst all of them is that there is some type of display of dominance, or you may even see a fight going on to determine who is the alpha of the group. The alpha male in the animal kingdom is usually the one who has managed to demonstrate to the entirety of the tribe that he is the strongest, healthiest and most capable of leading them. Generally, with animal groups, the males will attempt to win over the females by some type of display of strength. This is how the female determines which male she would like to be impregnated by. This display of strength also involves certain body language. These males want to show that they are the strongest. In order to do so, they will puff out their chest and keep their arms/wings wide in an effort to take up as much space as possible. They will keep their head up high, their eyes wide and they will walk with purpose and weight in their steps. The female animals take note of this body language, along with examining the colors of their feathers or fur to determine their level of health. This information allows her to choose which male she would like to have her babies. This can be observed- to a much lesser degree of course- in the human species as well. Humans tend to be attracted to the fittest, healthiest looking person and much of this comes down to body language as well. While it is not always a female choosing a male to have children with as it is in the animal kingdom, there is a similar form of mate selection that can be observed in a bar on a Friday night. Imagine having to attract the mate you want solely using body language and not your words. This may make things much more difficult.

*C*ase Study #2

A new teacher arrives at your school on the first day. This is her first teaching job and she has just graduated from a small university. She grew up in a small town and has just moved to a new city for this position. What advice would you give her, based on what we can extrapolate from knowing a few things about her background?

*T*his first day could either go very well or very challengingly for this new teacher. In order to maintain order in the classroom, it is important to demonstrate a level of authority. Someone coming from a small town and entering their first class of students may not have much experience or knowledge in demonstrating confident and leadership style body language. The first impression that the students make of this teacher could set the tone for the rest of the year. It is important to walk into the classroom with the shoulders back, the eyes up and scanning, the facial expression relaxed and comfortable, and the feet taking purposeful and big steps. Walking into the classroom with the shoulder hunched, the eyes down and the body stiff and shuffling will show to the class that you are nervous and will not be comfortable commanding the room. Walking in a certain way, however, will show the class that you are confident, secure and relaxed, and unafraid. Well before you have said a word to your new class of students, they will have examined you in order to determine what they will be able to get away with. While it isn't necessary to conduct your classroom in a strict way from here forward, the first thirty seconds are crucial.

Case Study #3

Our third case study involves a promotion. There are two employees that perform the same role in a corporate office environment. One of them is confident and self-assured. He walks into the office with his head held high and is quite talkative. He has a good rapport with the majority of the workers in the office and he maintains a positive work environment. When he takes a phone call he can be heard throughout the office as he speaks at a high volume and with a deep voice. The other employee is an extremely hard worker. He is quiet and shy, but he gets to work on time each day and he works silently with focus all day long. He has never taken a sick day in his 2 years at this company and often works through lunch. He has not had many one-on-one conversations with his boss as he works in a self-directed manner and does not need much guidance. Which of these two employees will get the promotion?

. . .

*W*hile the majority of people would like to believe that hard work demonstrates knowledge and skill and this will show itself, the silent hard worker who lacks confidence more often than not goes unnoticed. While it is a shame, in most cases we cannot focus all of our time on our work in order to show our bosses that we deserve the next promotion. What our employers want to see is an ability to work a room, to display our knowledge in an engaging manner. While the second worker silently devotes himself to his work, his boss is noticing the more confident and more demonstrative employee who makes a point to start conversations with him each morning and tell him the latest work-related knowledge he has gained. As unfortunate as it may be, we must be able to make ourselves noticed. This involves using our body language to our benefit. If we seem reserved and shy, we will not be entrusted with representing the company's image at a conference for example. The employee who demonstrates confident body language including a confident tone of voice will gain listeners over the employee who is quiet but knowledgeable. We must work on the balance of confidence and skill in order to progress to where we want to be.

*C*ase Study #4

Your son Jonathan is leaving for school one morning and you are saying goodbye to him at the door. You ask him if he completed all his homework and he assures you that he has. You examine his body language and notice that he is sweating on his upper lip and his brow. He is also fidgeting with his backpack straps. He is looking around quickly from side to side and avoiding eye contact. Is Jonathan lying?

. . .

$\mathcal{I}$t is safe to say that from the demonstration of nervous and fidgety behavior that Jonathan has not, in fact, completed his homework but is afraid of getting in trouble. He is telling a lie that he is unable to convince himself is true because it is quite black and white.

CONCLUSION

At this point in the book, you have gained all of the knowledge and skills that you need to be able to analyze people for a variety of reasons. Whatever brought you to this book, you will surely be walking away from it having learned a great deal about humans in general and also about yourself. Now, it is time for you to put what you have learned into practice and begin reaping the benefits!

How To Apply This To Real Life Scenarios

After reading this book, I urge you to study the people around you and practice analyzing everyone you encounter. At first, you may just begin by analyzing everyone's eyes- they have a lot to tell us. As you become more comfortable you can start taking your analyses further and eventually examine the entire person as a whole. Once you have become comfortable with this, you can practice it everywhere and I am sure you will see the benefits of it begin to show in your life and in your interactions.

Studying human behavior can be so interesting- as you may find nuances or differences in people from the area in which you live when compared to others. Use these techniques to achieve your dreams and goals by more efficiently using your time and energy and by putting forth the best first impressions that you can. You will no longer spend time trying to determine why you do not trust a person or why you felt something you couldn't explain when you met someone for the first time. Further, you will be able to enter professional scenarios with utmost confidence as you will be able to read other people and you will be able to anticipate how they will read you.

In Conclusion

I'd like to congratulate you for your commitment and discipline in finishing this book. Remember, the more you practice, the more naturally this will come to you. If you are someone who hasn't really practiced anything like this before, you may need to do it for a few months before you begin to analyze people automatically. If you are someone who is already somewhat skilled in this department, you may tune it up even more to read deeper into a person's behavior. Again, I want to thank you for your commitment and discipline in reading this book. I truly believe that the topics taught will help you advance your life in numerous ways.

While you are practicing all the topics you learned from this book, you are also growing your emotional intelligence. Some people have higher EI while others have lower EI. Luckily, EI is something that can be grown when you practice enough. By learning how to analyze others, you are growing your EI as you are paying more attention to the emotions and feelings of the person you are communicating with. EI is crucial in our modern world nowadays and is a trait that many employers seek within their hiring practices. Begin by working on your own emotional intelligence level, which will help you to understand and analyze other people more effectively.

This is a skill that can be practiced, honed and developed over your lifetime and this begins today! Work on fine-tuning this skill over your life and you will become an expert in no time. By taking the first step and reading this book, you are already miles ahead of most people.

NLP
SECRETS

Using NLP Techniques to Reprogram
Yourself & Others

Nadine Watson

INTRODUCTION

Congratulations on purchasing *NLP* and thank you for doing so.

Have you ever wished that your mind came with an instruction manual? Perhaps you felt like you would be greatly benefitted by being able to see the ways in which you talk to other people change. Maybe you feel like you need to figure out a way that you are able to better deal with some problems that you have. Maybe you realized that, ultimately, what you need to do is make some very big changes in the way that you see the world, but you are unsure how you can do that.

Thankfully, despite the complicated nature of the human mind, there are ways that you are able to figure out how best to sort of tap into your mind. You can learn how you can better take on the world. You can come up with the best possible ways in which you can control yourself. You can learn to tap into your own mind. You can discover the ways in which you can use the natural programming in your mind to sort of influence the way that you will behave. You can literally program yourself with methods such as neurolinguistics programming.

This book will teach you to do exactly that. You will learn how you can access your unconscious mind—the part of your mind that acts as the sort of driving factor behind everything that you do. You can use this part of your mind to discover how to better motivate yourself. You can tell your mind how better to respond, and by learning to do so in a way that your mind is receptive to, you know that you are taking back your control in the most meaningful way possible. All you have to do is learn that language of programming that your brain will require you to use.

Generally speaking NLP has a root in therapeutic use. It was created to allow for a practitioner, who has no formal psychology training, but has been trained in the art, to guide a patient or a client through learning how to reprogram their own mind. It works by tapping into the mind, identifying problems with the programming, and then learning to rewrite that programming to allow yourself to better cope with the problems that you are having.

We will go through this book first taking a look at how to define NLP in the first place. We will go over the most compelling benefits that you can use to take control of your mind. We will take a look at the ways in which it is commonly used, as well as which contexts you are likely to find it. We will take some time to talk about essential principles and other information that is necessary for you to know. At that point, we will start to dive into how NLP really works. We will look at mind mapping as the primary component that drives basically all of your perceptions of the world. We will take a look at the unconscious mind, especially in regards to NLP, where it plays a major role.

From there, it is time to get down to business. You will be guided through how NLP can be used for yourself to help yourself, and then as well as how it can be used to program other people in many different contexts. You will see how NLP can become the key into just about anyone else's mind, so long as you are able to make use of the fact of rapport to tap into it. You will be guided through understanding the various sensory cues that people use, and finally, you will be guided through the use of several NLP techniques for you and for those around you.

No matter who you are, or what your story is, or how you have gotten to the point that you are in your life, there are ways that you can overcome it. You can learn to take back control, little by little. You can learn how to be in charge of your own reactions and responses to the world around you, bit by bit. You can discover precisely what it takes to regain control of yourself by tapping into your mind, or to take control of other people by tapping into theirs as well. The end results can be incredible if you know what you are doing, and this book will help you with exactly that. You will learn how you can take control of yourself once and for all with the concepts that are provided within this book. All you have to do is read it.

NEURO-LINGUISTIC PROGRAMMING

AT SOME POINT IN TIME, you have probably wished that you could change yourself. You may have had a horrible habit that you wanted to be rid of. You may have had a desperate need to improve your own ability to be motivated to keep yourself on track and doing what you need to be. It could be that you are constantly finding yourself in bad situations because you cannot change your way of thinking to get yourself out of it. These habits can all become so deeply ingrained that it is impossible to imagine that you have some sort of way out. It is impossible to imagine a world in which you are able to find a way to escape the problem when that problem is all you have ever known. When your habits are familiar, they are more or less compelling to you. You will not see any sort of alternative because you will not see a way in which you could truly avoid them.

There is good news—just as you can fall into bad habits over time, you can learn new ones. You can learn how to pick up on the way that you tend to interact with the world. You can figure out the way in which you are acting and you can learn to retrain yourself. This is hardly a new concept in the world. It has been seen heavily in all sorts of other contexts. Cognitive behavioral therapy, a common form of psychotherapy that is touted for having quick results without much effort, has been lauded in recent years for its ability to engage in what is called cognitive restructuring—a way of literally rewiring the mind. Other therapies have similar concepts as well.

NLP has its own principles that it is able to use to get a very similar effect. If you have something that you are afraid of, NLP can help you reframe the thoughts surrounding it. If you have a habit that you oftentimes fall into, such as a bad habit that you engage in with other people or how you are constantly able to push them away, there is a great chance that you can change those habits with NLP as well.

There are many different methods that you can use that will help you. Whether you have anxiety, depression, anger problems, or some other problem that is underlying everything, NLP works to seek out that problem, identify that problem, and then figure out how to address that problem with ease. It does this to ensure that, at the end of the day, you can defeat your problems. It is designed to give you many different sorts of coping mechanisms that you can use to ensure that, at the end of the day, you are better able to protect yourself and change your mind. It is designed so that, at the end of the day, you are better able to ensure that your thought processing is something that is going to benefit you and ensure that you are successful in all of your endeavors.

. . .

*W*hen you become proficient in using NLP, you are able to look at how your brain works and how you can program your brain to work for you. You are able to rewrite your mindset that you have, working with the way that your brain naturally works as opposed to constantly attempting to override it. If you can get these processes just right, you are usually able to ensure that your mind will work better for you. You usually are able to overcome your problems. You usually are able to ensure that you have a mindset of a winner, and this all happens because you understand the language of your mind.

*I*ntroducing Neuro-Linguistic Programming

One of the most fundamental components of NLP is the acknowledgment that you are not in control of the world around you. You cannot control whether the car of the person next to you is going to veer suddenly into your lane. You cannot control whether some random person is going to choose to vandalize your home overnight. You cannot control whether your child is going to listen to you and go to bed on time tonight. You cannot control the world around you. In fact, you cannot fully control anything that is external from you. If it is not a part of you or your being, it is not within your complete and utter control. You must be able to accept this fact—you must be willing and able to ensure that you are able to put up with this. You must be able to see that, at the end of the day, you must accept that you cannot control everything—but that there are many areas within your life that you are in control of. When you can acknowledge what you can control as opposed to what you cannot, you can change your way of thinking. You can ensure that, at the end of the day, what you are doing is much better than what it would have been otherwise. You can fix your mindset into something that is easier to control and easier to create the right kinds of behaviors that you were hoping to engage in. When it comes right down to it, if you want to be able to find those mindsets that matter the most to you, you must be able to use your mindset to make it happen.

*E*ssentially, the foundation of this concept is that you have thoughts, feelings, and behaviors. They are constantly locked together. This is a fundamental principle of many different behavioral therapies that you are likely to find these days, and NLP latches onto it as well. When you make use of these methods for yourself, you are able to begin to control yourself, all thanks to the fact that you understand the intricate workings of the mind. Essentially, any thoughts that you have about something will create feelings. Those feelings influence the way that you behave, and most of the time, those behaviors then work in some way to reinforce the initial thought that you had. They all flow together to create a problem that you will have to tackle to defend yourself and ensure that, at the end of the day, you will be able to control yourself.

*N*LP makes heavy use of this-- you will see that the thoughts that you have are usually spawned by the experiences that you have developed at some point in time or another. It is likely that something that has happened to you has caused you to develop that thought, whether you went through a trauma or whether it was enjoyable. No matter what, however, the end result is the same: You wind up with a thought that underlies everything else. That thought will influence the behaviors that you have when involving that thought.

. . .

*L*et's put this into context for a moment. Imagine that you were in a bad car accident with a drunk driver. You were both fine, but you had a lengthy recovery at the hospital and permanently have an injured knee as a result. Your knee will always hurt and there is nothing that you can do about it. Now, as a result of the accident, you have a terrible association with driving. Your mind associates driving with the pain and the fear of the accident. It associates everything with the problems that came after the fact—the year of physical therapy trying to fix your knee, the attempts to recover, the medical bills, and everything else. All of this was highly unpleasant, and even if you are incredibly grateful that you survived, you must also remember that, at the end of the day, your unconscious mind is not looking at that. You do not see a car and think that you are lucky to be alive. Rather, you look at the driver's seat and imagine the accident.

*T*his sort of trauma happens after accidents or other traumatic incidents. You then get stuck in that sort of negative mindset. You cannot get past those negative beliefs that hold you back. You constantly have those negative thoughts pop up for you each and every time you attempt to live with the situation at hand. Perhaps, as soon as you get into a car, you immediately have those thoughts that you had when you were recovering. You cannot help it—it is just the way that your brain has hardwired itself.

*H*owever, you can learn to control it. NLP recognizes that your thoughts are incredibly powerful. You can tell that thoughts are powerful just by looking at the effect of placebo trials for medicine. Some people, who get that placebo medication that is nothing more than a sugar pill, report that they did see their symptoms improve. They report that they were better able to control the way that they thought. This effect is common to be found, and is so common that when you go into labor, or you see someone fighting cancer and getting chemo or radiation, they are told that their positive mindset is crucial. They must *believe* that it will work and that they will get better. They must believe that at the end of the day, they can recover and that in recovery, they will be able to thrive. When that happens, and when they accept the truth, that they are able to survive, they are so much more able to cope.

*N*LP focuses on that principle. It is honed in on making sure that the individual getting treatment is able to create positive, empowering beliefs that underlie everything. When there is a layer of positivity underneath everything, they are much better able to recover. Your positive beliefs that you can create will influence your behavior. If you think that you can actually do something, you are much more likely to do it. You will naturally put your all into it because you believe that it is something that you can do. You will be able to shift your way of thinking like this to ensure that, at the end of the day, you are better able to cope. You will find that, at the end of the day, you are able to take control of yourself and your mind—you just need to learn how to do that.

*T*he Mind, the Body, and You

NLP recognizes the fact that at the end of the day, there is a very close link between the mind and the body. Together, the mind and the body come together to create you. They are two halves of the whole you, like two sides of the same coin that are intricately linked but inherently different. You have both the mind and the body and they both work together to create your experiences.

*T*he mind is typically broken down into two pieces. It is your conscious mind—the part that you can control—and the unconscious mind—which you cannot. Both parts of the mind are incredibly important and yet, they cannot properly communicate together. They are constantly attempting to connect to each other. They are constantly attempting to get in alignment, but all too often, you tell yourself one thing but the unconscious mind produces the exact opposite result. Imagine, for example, that you desperately want to drive again after your accident. Well, your mind may assume that your desire to drive is not actually a desire to drive, and instead, it creates those feelings of fear. You fear driving because your unconscious mind, with the current paradigm that it has developed, makes you fear it. This means that, when you get behind the wheel, you are immediately overcome by that fear. Instead of being able to see that your fear is overwhelming you and overcoming it, you are behaving fearfully. Your unconscious mind does not understand that it is not giving you what it wants, and if it understood what you were asking of it, it would be able to do so.

*T*he way to the unconscious mind, however, is a tricky one. It is oftentimes through the body. You can begin to understand what the unconscious mind is thinking or doing by stopping to look at the body language of an individual—including yourself. You can learn to recognize the body language that will guide you; you can learn to see that, at the end of the day, the way in which you move or act is actually one that is highly dependent upon the way in which you act. You can usually figure out the way that your unconscious mind thinks by seeing what it does to the body language that you are using, and likewise, you can contact the unconscious mind through the use of body language as well.

*I*n fact, this happens regularly with the use of NLP—you will see both mirroring and the pace and lead techniques. These two techniques are highly dependent upon body language. You will see how rapport comes about through body language. You will see that anchoring is often done through body language as well.

*T*he body language that you have is typically read by the unconscious mind. It is an unconscious form of communication from person to person and when you can acknowledge that it is unconscious, you can then begin to better tap into it. You can see the ways in which you need to change your actions. You can see how you can interact with other people in a way that is effective. Ultimately, all you have to do is figure out the right way in which you can achieve that bridge.

*N*euro-Linguistic Programming Defined

Ultimately, NLP, then, can be broken up into three key processes that define it. You must consider these three namesakes carefully to truly understand what it is that NLP is and what it has to offer.

. . .

*N*euro refers to the wiring within the brain. It is a direct reference to the nervous system and the brain. It is how we process the senses that we have and encompasses all five of our natural senses. This part of the word is essentially how we sense the world around us. It is our experiences—it is how we process them. It is the way in which you physically processed that car accident or that awkward interview or the feelings that you had when you got into an argument with someone. It is some sort of way that your body perceives the way that your external world has interacted with you.

*L*inguistic then, refers to the communication system. This is how your unconscious mind assigns value to those senses and experiences that you have endured. These are the very words, feelings, pictures, and other senses that you use to associate and give meaning to the world around you. It could be that you define something as bad, or that you immediately feel like your knee hurts again when you see a car because you associate the sight of a car with pain. This is a majorly important point to consider and becomes the point that we try to change when you are looking into the process of using NLP in the first place.

*P*rogramming refers to the use of all of that information. It is the way in which you communicate within yourself. It may be that your unconscious mind sees a car and quietly leaves you feeling anxious, which then leads to you having a panic attack at the idea of getting in. It could be the way that you tell yourself that you dislike yourself or the way that you behave. It is everything else that is going on within your body. It is how you communicate with yourself and with other people. It is meant to help you achieve a goal of some sort. In the anxiety instance, it could be that the end goal is to help you stay safe. Your mind thinks that you want to stay safe, so it makes you afraid, and that keeps you out of a car—which is what got you into trouble in the first place.

*W*hen it comes right down to it, then, NLP takes into consideration the culmination of your senses, your words that you use to describe what you are going through, and the way that you respond to the world around you. All of this is thrown together to create the end result of you and your behaviors. It also looks at the fact that, out of all of that, you do have some degree of control—particularly over the linguistic portion of what is happening to you. You can change the way that you think about the world so you can then change the way that you behave in the world. When you learn to take control of how you feel, you can then ensure that you can better deal with just about anything. You can defeat your negativity. You can take back control. You can make sure that your programming aligns with what you want it to become.

THE BENEFITS OF NLP

WHEN IT COMES RIGHT DOWN to it, NLP can offer endless benefits to you. When you learn how to control the way that you think, you can influence so much of what you are doing, and that is something that you should remember to take control of. The fact that you learn how you can better control yourself means that you are able to ensure that, at the end of the day, you are the person that you want to be. You can teach yourself to go through life following the patterns of thought that matter to you. You can ensure that, at the end of the day, you will be prepared for anything that is thrown your way, and that is powerful. That is something that you can make total use of to ensure that you do live the life that you want.

*W*ithin this chapter, however, were are going to get more specific. We are going to delve into the many different ways in which NLP is beneficial to people as a whole. Whether you are applying the NLP techniques to yourself or those around you, you must keep in mind that, at the end of the day, they still hold true. Keep these in mind for ways that you could potentially make use of NLP to benefit yourself or to help you understand the ways in which you could use these methods if you were to need some sort of inspiration.

It Can Clear Your Vision

When it comes right down to it, NLP can help you clear your vision. Not your physical vision—but rather, it can help you learn how to focus on what you really want. It clears your aspirational sights. You are able to clearly understand what it is that you truly want in life. You are able to point at the goals that you hope to achieve and you can apply them to your everyday life. You can begin to make sense of those subconscious patterns that will exist within the way that you behave, and when you understand those, you can begin to apply them as well.

In particular, when you learn to use NLP, you can focus on goals that are aligned with a very specific purpose and when you make use of these methods, you can usually ensure that it actually happens for you. You can usually ensure that, at the end of the day, you can better control yourself. You learn that you can better understand the ways in which you interact with both yourself and with those around you. You learn that you can operate within that goal that you want—and because you will have a goal that you have had to articulate, you will be more likely to achieve it in the first place.

It Can Help You Overcome Your Limiting Beliefs

We all, to some degree or another, have limiting beliefs.

These are negative beliefs that do nothing but hold us back. It could be a belief that you are useless, for example; it could be that your belief is that you are unable to succeed at what you wish to do in life. it could be that your belief is something else entirely— but whatever it is, it is limiting you. Let's go back to that example involving the hypothetical car accident. After the accident, the limiting belief will have been something that was directly related to the accident itself. It will be that underlying thought that is keeping you back from being able to get into the car again. It will be that belief that is underlying everything that you are doing, keeping you from being able to better control yourself. It is that belief that you will be going through all sorts of problems that are not going to serve you well.

*N*o matter what your limiting belief is, however, NLP can teach you how to overcome it. NLP will focus on reframing that current belief in some way. This is typically done through the use of changing the meaning that you assign to what is happening. It is changing the way that you talk about these situations. When you change this, you are engaging with the linguistic portion of NLP, but in doing so, you are able to better defeat the negativity that is holding you back. It helps you figure out how you can change your mindset just enough to ensure that, at the end of the day, you are more in control. It ensures that, at the end of the day, you are better able to provide these for yourself to change everything about the way in which you view the world, enabling you to make the changes that you will need in life.

*I*t Can Make You Self-Confident

The way in which you engage with NLP will also work

well to aid in self-confidence issues. Many people, especially when their mindsets are already so incredibly negative, already suffer from low self-esteem. However, because you will be able to take control of yourself, you will be able to move forward in life with confidence. You understand that you will be able to change yourself and your thoughts. You understand that, at the end of the day, you can better control yourself. You understand that you are able to ensure that, at the end of the day, you are the only one that is in control of yourself, and you make use of that entirely. You take control of yourself. You ensure that you are the one that holds onto your own beliefs. You ensure that you are responsible for those mindsets that you take and how you allow them to control you.

*A*s the end result, you then understand that you can trust yourself to do what is right. You trust that, at the end of the day, you can ensure that you are making the right decisions. You can do this with ease, and in doing so, you guarantee that you are better suited to controlling yourself.

*T*his confidence can also be anchored, which is a method of teaching yourself how you can trigger yourself to feel something on a whim. You can essentially take control of the way in which you interact. You can force the point. You can make it so that you do decide that you should act in those manners and that helps you greatly.

*I*t Can Help You Manage Relationships with Difficult People

Another key point to remember is that when you make use of NLP, you learn how to understand yourself. You are learning to understand that oftentimes, the way in which we engage with other people is important to consider and that you can choose not to react to people with that same visceral anger that you may once have. We all have people in our lives that we do not like, whether they are people that we have to see regularly at work or people that we only see occasionally. No matter the situation, however, it is crucial that you understand how you can best deal with yourself. When you understand how to cope with yourself and how to best deal with your own emotions, you can essentially reframe the way that you see the people in your life, including those that used to annoy you. You can learn to tolerate them, and in doing so, you can usually also learn to respect them better.

Further, NLP is all about encouraging the development of rapport—that very important, essential technique that you will require to ensure that, at the end of the day, you are able to control the way in which you behave. When you look at NLP, you are better able to see that typically, you can learn how to connect with people that are difficult, and you can also use those methods to build up a rapport with someone else that may not like you. This can aid you greatly in ensuring that you can facilitate a good relationship with them as well.

It Can Help You Lead

NLP is also great for any sort of leader. If you are going to be leading or controlling other people in any sort of aspect at all, being able to understand and utilize NLP is a great way to ensure that you are developing the right abilities that will help you. You are able to develop the abilities that you will need to ensure that other people see you as worthy of respect. You develop the abilities that you need to ensure that people around you start to recognize that, at the end of the day, you are worthy of that respect by developing your own rapport with them. Further, you are also able to develop the ability to read other people, understand where they are coming from, and also be able to ensure that, at the end of the day, you can better cope with the way that you deal with other people as well. These processes lend themselves heavily to a leadership position and by mastering them, you can ensure that you are better positioned to lead effectively.

It Can Help You Problem Solve

The use of NLP is all about creative thinking. It is about taking a problematic thought and then thinking of a way that you are able to think about it differently. It is being able to see a dog and decide that actually, you are going to think about it differently and instead of defining it as a dog, you are going to define it as a four-legged household domestic mammal that is also known as man's best friend. When you change the way that you get around defining something, you are able to then change the reaction that you have to it, and that is precisely what it is that NLP wants to do.

Those skills, however, also lend themselves well when it comes to creative problem-solving. You learn to identify the way of thinking to find different patterns, and that ability can also become extrapolated and used to help benefit other situations as well. You can look at the way that you can solve other problems as well with these methods. You can learn how you can develop new strategies and new approaches to a situation because of the resilience that you develop with these processes.

It Can Help You Control Your Mindset

Along those same lines, then, you must also consider the fact that, when you use NLP, you are able to control your own mind. You are able to take utter control over those areas in your life that you once believed to be entirely out of your grasp, such as your thoughts and your feelings. Many people regard feelings to be entirely out of your control because they are automatic and instinctive. While that may be the case, it is also important to remember that, at the end of the day, your feelings themselves are really only the product of your thought processes that you are having at any point in time. When you keep that in mind, you can understand that you can control your mindset and your emotions. You have the freedom to create the emotions and the motivation that you will need to ensure that you get the results that you need at the end of the day. When you are able to change the development of these thoughts and improve upon yourself, you will find that you will greatly better yourself and that is very important to remember.

It Can Help You Break Bad Habits

We all have bad habits at one point in time or another. It could be that you bite your nails. It could be that you reach for the bottle whenever you have a bad day at work. It could be that you have a tendency to mindlessly snack through the day. No matter what that bad habit that you have is, it becomes important to recognize that you do have some degree of control over it. You can learn how you can defeat those negative behavioral patterns for yourself and ensure that your bad habits are entirely defeated.

When you can do that, you can ensure that you are not wasting your time, your efforts, your money, or anything else. You ensure that you are living the life that you want to live and that is a huge deal at the end of the day.

*W*hen it comes right down to it, your bad habits are just unconscious thoughts that are being acted out. You can learn to identify the thought, reframe it, and then take control of the problem that you are facing or the bad habit that you engage in. When you do that, you are able to make use of all sorts of techniques that you can use to break these habits—permanently.

It Can Better Your Relationships

Because of the simple fact that you are spending time learning to understand how you work yourself, you are able to ensure that you develop the healthy habits that you will want to encourage and facilitate to ensure that your body and mind are able to also facilitate positive relationships. Making use of this will greatly help you understand that, at the end of the day, you can take control. It will ensure that, at the end of the day, you are in complete and utter control of what you are doing, how you do it, and how you want to do it. This means that you can ensure that the habits that you develop are healthy, beneficial, and will help ensure that your relationships are better than ever. They grow stronger, facilitated by your better habits.

*I*t **Can Improve Your Ability to Communicate**

The fact that you will be so incredibly focused on your internal communication also prepares you to be able to better understand the communication with other people as well. This means that, at the end of the day, you would be able to better understand the ways in which you interact with other people. You would be able to see that, at the end of the day, the communication that you have does not just impact you—it also impacts the way that you communicate with other people, which directly influences them as well.

This awareness means that you can better communicate what really matters to you. It means that you can better communicate the way in which you engage with other people. It means that at the end of the day, you can ensure that you are better able to get your message across in a way that is important to you. It will ensure that, at the end of the day, you do communicate effectively, a skill that is necessary in every aspect of your social life, and you will be sure to develop that with NLP as your guide.

It Can Help You Help Others

You can also begin to help other people, too. You can learn how you can best motivate those around you, identifying their strengths and weaknesses so you can be better prepared to help them. You are able to work to improve on those crucial coaching skills that will greatly influence them. This means that you are able to keep people around you motivated. You learn how you can begin to reframe the thoughts of other people as well, something that is highly beneficial to you. You will be able to ensure that, at the end of the day, you are capable of recognizing the way in which your words can change what is going on for other people as well, allowing that access to understanding their minds and their motivations.

· · ·

*B*ecause you will have this ability, you will know that you have the capability of helping other people in all sorts of contexts. You can help them find the truth behind their biggest problems. You will have the ability to better understand the way in which they are dealing with other people as well. When you master this, you know that you are better able to encourage those around you to change their thinking around as well and that is highly beneficial.

*I*t Can Help You Understand Others

You will also be able to understand other people—and that means that you can mimic them as well. This is known as modelling—you are able to look at people that can do what you want to do, whether personally or professionally, and you can begin to model them. You can begin to understand what it is that is bringing them to that success that you are looking for and when you can do that, you know that, at the end of the day, you will be able to become more successful on your own just by default.

*I*t Can Help Cope with Changes

You will also be more prepared to deal with any changes that you face at any point in time as well. This means that you will be able to ensure that, at the end of the day, you are more adaptable. You are able to become more flexible as a direct result of the fact that you can alter your thinking. You are able to change the view that you may have on a difficult situation. Instead of only seeing the bad in a situation, you can find the good that is hidden there as well. Instead of only seeing the problems that you face, you will also see how you can change the way that you interact with those that you are surrounded by. You can ensure that you are prepared, no matter what happens, to cope, and the NLP methods that you master will help you ensure that that is actually the case.

*I*t Can Lead To Better Work Performance

On another, less personal note, you can also make use of NLP in the workplace as well. It can be a powerful asset when it comes down to managing teams of people around you that will need to be motivated and influenced. It allows you to ensure that those that you work with are kept in a positive mood which can influence their productivity as well. It ensures that you can boost team performance at work, allowing you to run a tighter ship and ensure that everyone on board said ship is functioning effectively and doing what needs to be done.

*I*t Can Make Sales Jobs Easier

Finally, one last benefit to consider is specific to sales jobs, though you could expand it to include anyone that has to ever negotiate anything. When you are prepared to negotiate anything at all, you know that you are able to better understand everything that is going on. You are prepared to be able to negotiate clearer than ever because you will be able to implement all of the various skills that you require to use in your setting. You will be able to ensure that, at the end of the day, you can better deal with people. You will better understand them through developing that experience working with the unconscious mind. You will be able to ensure that, at the end of the day, you can better deal with these people with ease if you know what you are doing. When it comes right down to it, you are able to ensure that you can also be more persuasive just because you know how to frame things in a way that will be persuasive at the end of the day. You will be able to better cope with the way that you interact with other people and that is highly powerful. When you know what you are doing, you ensure that you are capable of better implementing your own techniques to benefit you and to benefit your attempt to negotiate.

*T*his does not mean that you are intentionally steamrolling over someone, however—you are usually attempting to find a way in which you can better interact with people. You are ensuring that, at the end of the day, you can ensure that you are getting everyone onto the same page so you can all come to a fair agreement. You are able to understand better what they want so you can ensure that you are attempting to meet those needs in any way that you possibly can. When you can do all of this and more, you can usually ensure that you are more successful in the way that you interact with those around you and that is highly powerful.

USING NLP

AT THE END of the day, NLP is able to be used in a wide range of contexts. It is used highly in many different scenarios, all with varying results. However, if you are interested in making NLP work for you, it is absolutely something that you can take control of. When you make use of NLP, you can ensure that you do better understand what is going on in your mind or the minds of others and that kind of insight into the human mind is highly powerful. For that reason, NLP could really be applied to any social situation. From parenting to relationships to negotiations, NLP could be a great asset in just about any situation.

*N*evertheless, within this chapter, we are going to tighten our scope. We are going to firstly look at what it is that NLP does and how it works. We are going to dive into that most basic foundation to better understand NLP before we begin to look at several of the most common applications. We will look briefly at how it can be used in medicine, as a therapy, to better the self, to manage other people, in negotiations, at work, in relationships, and we will briefly touch base about how it can be used in many manipulative situations as well. While manipulation is never condoned, many people have turned this tool, which is something that can do the world a lot of good, into something manipulative and harmful. That is a huge problem—that means that some people are naturally going to resist NLP already—they will see the negativity that surrounds it and do anything in their power to ensure that they are better able to control everything around them.

How NLP Works

Ultimately, there is one very simple equation that sums up how NLP works:

Input + Internal processes = Output

Essentially, your output, which is your behaviors and your emotions, is little more than a sum of your input and your internal processes. This simplifies things greatly, but it does a good job of making it understandable for a beginner. You begin with the input. That is the world around you. The input is anything that happens around you; it could be that it is your sense of taste, sight, or sound. Your input will always be the sensory data that your body is receiving—that is anything that is perceived by your senses at all. This comes in five key forms:

- **Kinesthetic:** This is any sort of sensory data that comes to you through the use of movement or touch. It is sensory data that comes from the body itself as opposed to any of the sensory organs that you will have. It could be temperature, a touch, a texture, or a movement. It is your ability to be aware of space and movements.

- **Visual:** This is your visual data that you receive. It is your sense of sight—anything that you receive from your eyes. It could be something that is in front of you, words on a page, a picture that you saw, a video that you watched, or anything else that was primarily understood through the use of your eyes.
- **Auditory:** This is the use of your ears or your sense of hearing. When you are exposed to the sounds of the world around you, you are usually working with auditory data.
- **Olfactory:** This refers to your sense of smell and data that you are able to receive about the world through the use of your nose.
- **Gustatory:** This is the use of your mouth and your sense of taste. When you taste something in the air or in your mouth, it is a gustatory stimulus.

Any input that you receive is going to be in one of those five forms. It defines the experiences that you encounter and your body logs them all throughout these senses. It is the way in which you are able to interact with the world. Your body must be able to make sense of it somehow, and that is primarily done through the use of your senses.

The senses are then controlled by the internal processes. The internal processes that you have are two-pronged—you have your filters, which are unconscious, and then you have your internal representations of the data that is being processed in your mind, which is also unconscious but usually drives how you behave strongly

NADINE WATSON

. . .

*T*he filters that you have are kind of like a giant sieve that your sensory data is filtered through. It is a culmination of everything that you have experienced in the past, which is being used to better understand the situation in front of you. It is essentially being able to understand the way in which you are able to recognize the world around you, based on past experience. Your unconscious mind is attempting to create that sort of hypothesis it can to understand what is going on. Remember, hypotheses are educated guesses made based on background data and if you do not have that background data, you cannot make that educated guess that you need to make. This means that you will naturally base the way that you see the world upon the way that it has been in the past. If you have been in a car accident before, you may be more inclined to avoid driving on days that you know are going to be full of drunk drivers, such as the 4th of July, New Years, Christmas, Thanksgiving, and the like. When you are able to create that generalization that people usually drive drunk on holidays, you then decide that you will not drive anywhere on the holiday. That is making use of the filters that you have.

*U*sually, filters will be defined as ways that you are able to generalize the sensory data. They include attitudes that you may have developed over time. They involve memories that you may have as well. They include the ways in which you are able to sort through the thoughts, and the values that you currently have. They involve the beliefs that you hold that will influence the way that you behave. They involve the strategies that you take to ensure that you are better able to control the way in which you engage with the world. They also include the use of the language that you use at the end of the day to describe what you are going

268

through. After getting filtered through the filters, your senses then go down to the internal representations that you have.

*A*t that point, you then have your output. The output that you usually develop is either through the use of emotions or the use of behaviors. Either are proper examples of output, and you can very clearly see the way in which experience and thought then influence the way that you behave and feel through this sort of chain.

*E*ssentially, then, NLP will change those filters or it will influence that internal representation that you are holding onto. By changing those, you are then able to change the way in which you behave. You change the internal processes to better suit what you need, and then the output changes with it, allowing you to successfully make use of NLP.

*N*LP and Medicine

NLP is sometimes touted as a way that you can cure all sorts of different diseases, including cancer, HIV, and other diseases that do require medical attention. While NLP is not a magical cure-all, it can be used to help fight off some of the mental effects of living with these long-term, chronic, or sometimes, even terminal diseases. When you are able to make use of NLP when you are critically ill, you can help yourself come to terms with the problem. You can make use of the ways in which you can better process the information. You can help with the mindset that you are holding to allow yourself to better deal with the problems that you are facing.

*K*eep in mind that NLP will NOT cure cancer. It will NOT cure HIV or AIDS or any other disease at all. It is not medicine itself. However, it is a very powerful tool, just like meditation, mindfulness, and all sorts of therapies that people make use of when they are ill. You can make use of NLP to be a helpful tool during your illness, but it should not be the primary form of treatment.

*N*LP and Psychotherapy

NLP is highly used in a psychotherapeutic approach. It was initially designed to be a new approach to psychotherapy that would allow for the use of less training to be used. It is able to be used to help in many issues that you would commonly go to a psychotherapist for, such as negative feelings, anxiety, depression, or other mental health issues. NLP is able to make use of treating all of these through the use of changing thoughts. It is supposed to be systemic, focused, and solution-focused, allowing you to be able to reframe thoughts that are not helping you.

*E*ssentially, NLP works much in the same way that many other solution-focused brief therapies aim to do—it works hard on getting people to acknowledge where problems lie so they can then ensure that they are fixing the problem. When they are able to fix the problem, then, they are able to begin seeing those behavioral changes that they are looking for. At the end of the day, you can better do this to help find the positive context in any situation, therefore allowing you to better deal with any problems that you may otherwise ordinarily face. It is usually quite effective thanks to the fact that it returns power right back to the individual. It allows the client or the individual that is making use of NLP to be able to treat themselves because they understand themselves and that alone is incredibly powerful. When you can make use of that yourself, you know that you are better able to ensure that you cope with anything that is going on around you. You know that you are capable of better coping with your problems on a regular basis and that is where NLP gets its power. When you learn to understand what you are going through and how to deal with it, you are better prepared in the long run to cope with everything that you are dealing with.

NLP and Bettering the Self

As we have talked about repeatedly so far, one of the more common uses of NLP, at least on a personal level, involves bettering the self. When you focus on yourself and bettering yourself, you are usually able to change your own mindsets. You are empowered by the use of NLP to ensure that, at the end of the day, you can better cope with anything that you face. You can better deal with your problems because you can better influence the way that you think.

This means that NLP then becomes a powerful self-improvement tool. You can slowly eliminate all sorts of negative problems that you may otherwise struggle with. You can learn to eliminate that negativity to ensure that, at the end of the day, you do live a life that you value. You can ensure that you do live a life that is highly supportive of everything that you want, such as ensuring that you can better control the ways in which you deal with your problems. You can eliminate problematic habits.

You can erase thoughts that are sabotaging yourself or your relationships with others. You can effectively teach yourself to be the person that you have the potential to become.

$\mathcal{N}$LP and Managing Others

NLP is also commonly used in managerial situations. It can be used to help influence other people, as we have discussed. It can be used to ensure that, at the end of the day you do know how to motivate other people. You are able to play into team dynamics in just the right way to ensure that everyone around you is able to function accordingly.

$\mathcal{T}$he use of NLP and managing others becomes highly beneficial if you do work in any sort of a leadership role in which you need to be influencing the way other people work, whether that influence will play out in how you interact with them, how you approach situations or how you are able to keep people motivated. These all matter and you are able to ensure that your interactions with those around you are always efficient in making sure that everything does work out the way that they should.

$\mathcal{N}$LP and Negotiations or Persuasion

NLP also becomes a highly effective tool in negotiation, especially if the negotiations start off on a bad foot. If you notice that everyone around you is not really open to negotiations, you are able to make use of a lot of the methods of NLP to ensure that you can get people to open up and be willing to negotiate. You are usually able to do this with ease if you know what you are doing and if you can take control in these manners, you can ensure that the people around you are influenced in the right way to help with what you want. You can use methods such as the way that you frame your questions to naturally sway the way that people are thinking. You can use NLP to help yourself to frame the ideas or to ensure that you are tapping into the ways in which the other party sees the world around him or her. The powers of NLP can be highly effective when it comes right down to it if you know what you are doing and you ensure that you are able to encourage it.

NLP and Relationships

Likewise, in relationships, you are able to have high levels of influence with the use of NLP. You can usually ensure that you approach situations in ways that will naturally facilitate relationships to grow. You will be able to understand the ways in which those around you are working or interacting, meaning that you will be able to better work with them.

When you use NLP in your relationships, you are typically going to be doing so in ways that will help you to better communicate. You may tap into these techniques in ways that will give you that insight that you need to understand what is going on, how to understand the people that you are interacting with, and why you should do what you must do to convince them of something. It allows you to open up that connection and that feeling of connection between you and the other person. You will be able to better master those feelings of rapport and trust between you and those around you with the use of these methods and that can be highly powerful for you at the end of the day. All that matters is that you must ensure that you take the plunge and you make use of everything that you would need.

*N*LP and Manipulation

Finally, one last context that you will often find NLP in is the use of manipulation. This is one that is far more sinister than many of the others—it is for the sole benefit of the individual using the NLP in the first place. NLP is meant to be a tool for helping and for better growth. It is designed to be a helpful tool. It is meant to ensure that, at the end of the day, you can better interact with those around you, and yet, some people will take the same principles that are so incredibly powerful and persuasive, and they will turn it into a big tool to control the people around them. This is a huge problem and is part of the reason that NLP has such a bad reputation already.

*R*emember, NLP itself is not inherently a tool of manipulation. It is not inherently bad or good—it is nothing more than a tool. The way that it is used will determine the end result and if someone else chooses to use this tool in a way that is harmful, that is a problem with the individual user rather than a problem with the techniques themselves.

THE PRINCIPLES OF NLP AND OTHER ESSENTIAL INFORMATION

BEFORE WE START DELVING into more important information that will help prepare you to make use of the techniques that will be included within this book, you must first begin to understand the principles that guide NLP. These are a combination of the core concepts that you will see repeatedly throughout the book as well as the four key pillars that will frame the way in which you interact with NLP in the first place. The pillars themselves are quite powerful and they will help you to understand what the objectives behind your NLP usage should be. The concepts that you will be introduced to as well will show you precisely what it is that you will be targeting to better deal with the problems that you are facing.

This chapter is highly focused on further background information that will build the foundations for what you do. It is important for you to recognize the importance of what you are doing within this chapter so you can better understand everything that is going on. When it comes right down to it, you should make sure that you understand all of these concepts before you progress. If you cannot understand and remember these principles, you are going to struggle in later areas in this book and that can be a major problem for most people. Spend the time to really understand what is going on here. Make sure that you recognize what you are doing and how you are doing it. This is crucial for you to ensure that, at the end of the day, you will be successful in your endeavors.

The Pillars of NLP

Before we dive in, you must be aware that NLP, like any other concept or therapy, is built upon a foundation of background information. These are the concepts that will support what is going on—they give the field itself its focus, narrowing down what is being attempted. NLP is no different than any other field of thought or method of therapy—it is focused highly on several key concepts that, when they come into play, are able to highly guide the way in which you see the world. They influence the ways that you focus on what you see and what you do. They make you understand what is going on and ensure that you get what it is that NLP really wants to encourage.

NLP itself, for the practitioner, is highly focused on four key points that you will have to remember. If you can keep these four points in mind, you can ensure that you will be successful and you will ensure that you are able to make use of NLP. These are the four defining factors that you must keep in mind to ensure that you can influence those around you in the ways that you seek to do: Rapport, sensory awareness, outcome thinking, and behavioral flexibility.

· · ·

*R*apport

*T*he first pillar of NLP is rapport. Rapport itself is the foundation for everything else. If you do not have any rapport with someone else, you cannot hope to use NLP techniques with them. Rapport is sort of like that magic that keeps it working—it is the reason that you are able to control other people's thoughts and behaviors. It is essentially the measurement of trust between you and another person.

*R*apport is normally developed naturally over time. If you look at two people who are good friends, you can usually tell because of the body language. They are focused on each other and they engage in what is known as *mirroring*. This is the act of unconsciously following the lead of someone else's body language. It is actively changing the way that you behave to match the body language of someone else to better understand them. It is caused by the activation of mirror neurons—the neurons within the brain that activate when we see someone else doing something. It is essentially how we are able to understand them- it is our ability to empathize with other people and recognize the way in which they are feeling.

*G*enerally, the more rapport that you have with someone else, the more that you tend to empathize with each other, and that leads to the activation of the mirror neurons within the brain, leading to a higher tendency for the brain to mimic the behaviors of someone else.

. . .

*T*he next time that you are sitting at a restaurant, try to look at some of the people that you see. Look at the way that you see people who are clearly married or have been together for a long period of time tend to interact with each other. Watch how their very movements seem to be influenced by each other. Watch how when one takes a drink, the other one does moments later as well. This happens regularly—it is the way that you can tell that two people really trust each other.

*C*ompare that to a couple that is clearly awkwardly on a first date, not really understanding what they are doing or how they should do it or whether they even really like each other. Their behaviors will seem almost disjointed, as if they are on two different fields altogether.

*R*apport is that measurement that will help you to understand if you have been trusted. When you know it is there, it is easy to look at and understand. It becomes simple to be able to look at a situation, say that you can see where the rapport is showing and point out the ways in which you can better cope. It is great to be able to see the ways in which you can better deal with the situations that you are in. It can help you to under-stand if someone else is comfortable enough with you for you to attempt to use NLP techniques yourself.

*N*ow, we will be delving into rapport in more depth later in Chapter 9: Rapport, but for now, be aware that it is a major part of NLP, especially if you intend to use NLP techniques on other people. If you do intend to do so, you will need to make sure that you follow certain protocols that will be introduced later.

Sensory awareness

*T*he second key principle that serves as a pillar for NLP is the use of sensory awareness. It is the principle that recognizes that everything that you will be doing and every way that you will be interacting with other people is dependent upon the senses. You must be well aware of the way in which those around you are sensory aware. You must understand which of their senses they seem to favor and which they do not pay as much attention to. You must be willing and able to pay attention to everything that is going on around you.

*I*f you want to use NLP on someone else, you have a lot to consider. You must consider the environment that you would like to be in when you attempt to use it. You should consider the ways in which you interact with the people that you do interact with. You must understand the way in which you present yourself to the other person and align it with the way that they are going to be most likely to perceive. If you are using NLP for yourself, you must be aware of the ways in which you prefer to use your senses as well. You must know all of this so you can begin to influence yourself. You must be well aware of the ways that you interact with yourself and with the world around you so you can better cope with any problems that you may hit during this time.

· · ·

279

*Y*ou will also need to be able to identify nonverbal cues, either your own or those of someone else if you are attempting to make use of NLP for other people. All of this is crucial to remember—if you are able to focus on the ways that you can understand other people, you are usually able to also ensure that the body language used is also going to be effective.

*Y*ou can use this sensory awareness, for example, to identify when you are feeling angry or anxious about something. You can tap into your understanding of your body to see the way that you are feeling right that moment and to make it work for you. You can use it to see how other people are feeling as well. From there, you can then begin to look at the way that the environment is leading to those feelings in the first place. When you can identify that, you can better control what is going on and you can get valuable information that could be used later as well.

*O*utcome thinking

*O*utcome thinking is the third of the four pillars of NLP and it is, essentially, a goal. It is looking at every interaction and every attempt to use NLP as a chance in which you can meet a goal. It is attempting to find those goals that will drive you so you can lock onto them. Really, this is all about being able to ensure that your attempts to alter the way in which other people think are always intentional. It is your way of guaranteeing that when you are interfering with someone's mindset, whether your own or someone else's, you can tell the way in which it is relevant and why it matters. It is being able to ensure that you always have a purpose that is pushing you forward and driving what you are doing.

*M*any people make the mistake of not trying to drive themselves forward with a goal. They do not make sure that there is something that is reminding them to keep on moving forward and because of that, they fail. When you have a well-thought-out goal, you know precisely what it is that you are trying to change in someone else. You know exactly what matters —you know what you need to do to help yourself or those around you and you can then focus your reframing attempts to allow you to succeed at those goals.

*U*ltimately, your goal can be just about anything. That is something that you will have to determine for yourself. However, no matter what it is, you must make it a priority for yourself. You must make it a driving factor for yourself; it must become something that pushes you forward and you must put in the effort to ensure that both body and mind are able to achieve whatever it is that you are looking for.

*F*lexibility in behavior

*F*inally, the last principle, the last pillar of NLP is flexibility in your behavior. This essentially means that you need to have more than one plan at any point in time. You must be able to change the way that you interact with other people. You must be able to change the ways in which you better interact with those around you. You must ensure that, at the end of the day, you are able to make changes that you will need. You will be able to let go of the method that is not working for you when it does not work for you so you can then shift gears entirely. When that happens, you are then able to ensure that you do make the proper decisions to help yourself. You are able to ensure that you do change the way that you interact with the world or the client, or even yourself.

*W*hen you are able to focus on the ways in which you interact with the world, you are better able to direct yourself. You can make sure that you are flexible enough that you are always able to find a solution that will work for you—even if that solution is not the first, second, or third on your list. You are flexible enough to keep on trying, no matter what the problem is and no matter what it is that you would like to do instead.

*S*econdly, you are able to ensure that, no matter what it is that you are doing, you will be resilient. You are resisting that urge to completely and utterly ignore the chances that you will fail. You are able to ensure that, no matter what is going on with you, you will succeed, and the flexibility will help you.

*W*hen it comes to the human mind, you cannot be rigid. You must recognize that you have to make very serious changes. You have to recognize that you must be willing and able to look at the potential roadblocks that you will hit—and they will be there. You must be flexible enough to continue on despite the roadblocks. It is only then, when you are able to resist the urge to give up or resist the urge to ensure that you are going to let defeat win over you, that you are able to truly make these principles work for you.

Essential Concepts for NLP

Along with those fundamentals to NLP, there are also three core concepts that serve as essential points that you must also be well aware of when it comes to being able to alter the mind of someone else. These three components that you must remember are subjectivity, consciousness, and learning. If you can remember all three of these, you will be more likely to succeed at the attempts that you make. If you can remember these essential concepts, you know that you will be more likely to be able to interact with the minds of other people. These three concepts determine everything about our way through which we navigate through the world and they are essential to remember.

ubjectivity

ubjectivity is the idea that, at the end of the day, we all see the world through our own goggles. We all have our own unique perspectives on the way in which we see the world and you must be able to recognize that each and every person's individual perspective will be relevant to them in some way. You have your own personal view that you must remember and that will determine your own takeaway from a situation.

· · ·

*I*magine, for example, that you see the number 3 painted on the floor. If you were to slowly walk in a circle around the 3, you would see as it transforms from a 3 to an M to an E to a W, and then right back to a 3. This is because of the fact that from a different perspective, you will see something entirely different. This is the case when it comes down to the way in which people see their own experiences as well. When it comes right down to it, the way in which you experience the world is going to be highly dependent upon the way in which you see the world around you and what you have experienced beforehand.

*O*ur subjective realities, our maps that we create of the world around us and how we see them, are entirely built upon our senses and our experiences, which are also labeled by the way in which we talk about them. This is important to remember —when you look at your own perspectives, you will have your own behaviors that go along with them. You will have your own opinions and your own attempts at explaining what has happened.

*T*he way that you then experience what you experience will also influence the way in which you experience future events as well. That will also influence the way that you see future events. Imagine, for example, that your relationships have just failed. Your past relationships have all failed for one reason or another. The next time that you go into a relationship, you may then assume that you are going to fail again in some way. You may assume that you are naturally going to fail just because of the way that every other relationship so far has gone.

· · ·

*N*LP targets this fact—it targets the fact that everything is subjective to allow for the understanding that while everything is subjective, it is also plastic and malleable. Those subjective assumptions, because they are unique to everyone and they are formed over time, they can also be seen as easily rewritten as well.

*C*onsciousness

*T*he second aspect that serves as a key concept in NLP is consciousness. We have two forms of consciousness—the conscious and the unconscious. When it comes right down to it, the conscious mind is something that you are aware of. It is your active thoughts and feelings about something. Your unconscious mind, on the other hand, is out of your reach. It is automatic and it is constantly operating without any input from you. It makes patterns and then follows through with them without the input that you could have had.

*E*ssentially, the conscious mind is something that you can directly control, but if you want to rewrite the unconscious mind, it will require you to make use of other methods—which NLP is glad to do. We will be delving deeper into this concept in later chapters as well.

earning

. . .

*T*he last key concept to keep in mind is learning. This is the primary guiding factor that drives NLP. NLP is all about learning—either you are teaching people or you are learning from them. The rewriting that you are doing of the mind is all about you being able to learn something new, such as a new behavioral pattern or a new pattern of thinking. It could also be that you are trying to make someone else learn those new patterns of thinking.

*E*ssentially, this is the use of trying to develop better behaviors. Think about it—behaviors are learned. Many of the thoughts that you have are learned. Just about every aspect of who you are and what you do is *learned*. If all of the filters that you use to see the world are learned and all of the internal maps are learned, they are also rewritable, and that is where NLP comes into play. Essentially, it makes use of the learning process.

*I*n NLP, we refer to this as modeling—when you model something or someone, you mimic the behaviors. You may unintentionally drink from your cup at the same time as someone else. You may unintentionally follow the lead of someone else when you are walking. You may take on the same mood, the same behaviors, or the same thoughts as someone else. Essentially, NLP is all about learning.

*T*he learning that you go through throughout your life will help you to navigate through everything. You can make yourself learn how to rewrite your thoughts. You can choose to learn new thought patterns. You can ensure that the patterns that you do follow are those that are effective for you and that is what matters.

*I*f you are able to use this concept, you will be able to, for example, teach yourself that, at the end of the day, you will feel a certain way when you do a specific hand movement. You may teach yourself to recognize that your thoughts are not productive the way that they are. You may teach yourself that the car accident that you went through was not traumatic or that you are not upset by something that happened. Essentially, you are able to use learning to hijack the subjective mind, and that is how you are able to rewrite everything that goes on around you.

MAPS, THE MIND, AND NLP

AS WE HAVE ESTABLISHED at this point, the way that we understand the world determines everything. It determines how we interact with the world around us. It determines our emotions, our behaviors, and our tendencies. It controls everything that we are and everything that we do, all because the mental maps are there to guide us through it. These mental maps are exceedingly powerful, and to be able to control them is to, essentially, take control over the mind.

*W*ithin this chapter, we are going to consider this in-depth. We are going to look at the ways in which you can control the minds of other people, or of yourself. We are going to consider the fact that, at the end of the day, we are controlled by those mental maps that we live. We are going to determine the way that we see what we are doing and how we are able to fit within reality itself through the use of what are our mental maps. These are our navigators; they are the literal maps that we are able to follow throughout reality. They are the ways in

288

which we are capable of doing so much throughout our lives. They define the world around us and help us to understand everything that we are surrounded with, without worrying about the conscious effort that would have to go into it. After all, why should you have to stop, see a snake, and then consciously debate whether or not the snake could be dangerous? By the time that you have pondered the potential for danger or whether the snake is likely to be venomous, you could have already been bitten. For this reason, it is better to sometimes act first and think later when it comes down to questions of survival.

*T*his makes use of generalizations, which we are going to be considering heavily throughout this chapter. We are going to be looking at how those generalizations and those perceptions become the maps that we can use to navigate the world. We are then going to look at the relationship between mental maps that are created and using NLP, either on yourself or on someone else. As you read through this chapter, you will be guided through the way that people see the world. You will develop a better understanding of the ways in which other people are likely to interact with the world, and better understand even the ways in which you interact with yourself and the world around you.

Our Perceptions of Reality

In the world, we are constantly inundated by experiences in the form of sensory data. Your version of reality, from your position, no matter what that position is, is vastly different than that of someone standing next to you. It does not matter what it is, where you are, or who you are; the world will look different to you than it does for someone else. This is because your perspective is endlessly being shaped, sculpted, and molded into something new; it is constantly being influenced by what you see in the world around you and the ways in which you explore the world. When you keep that in mind, you know that, at the end of the day, you will be better able to understand the reasons that you look at the world; you just have to learn how to read the maps.

*Y*our senses are constantly taking in data. Although you may not be paying attention to it, there is a lot of data that you are constantly logging on the cusp of your awareness. The unconscious mind, which we will be discussing in the next chapter, is highly perceptive and is constantly aware of anything within your sensory perception. Even if you are not currently paying attention to it or focusing on it, you are still, at least unconsciously, aware that it is there. Think about it this way: Have you ever been talking to someone at a park, but suddenly ducked when a ball came flying at you? You may not have been aware of that ball consciously, but your unconscious mind was paying enough attention to your surroundings to get you to duck You could have also done this with a spider, a snake, or any other threats—you respond automatically to the world around you because of that unconscious mind.

*T*hese perceptions, however, can very quickly move above sensory into pattern recognition. Imagine that you are in a relationship with someone and you are constantly changing the ways in which you interact with the world in accordance to those the way in which your relationship goes. Perhaps your partner has a tendency of sighing loudly when you make a mistake, his shoulders sagging, and a look of annoyance or disappointment on his face every time that you say something that he disagrees with. While you may not have noticed it yourself, the unconscious mind is paying attention. The unconscious mind sees that you have this problem. It knows that, at the end of the day, your partner does this every time. You then come to associate making a mistake or misunderstanding something as being a disappointment to other people. This may not exist in your conscious mind and you may not even think about it; but, every time that you make a mistake, you tell yourself that you have disappointed those around you. You tell yourself that you have messed up and that you need to fix the way in which you interact with others, all without being conscious of it.

*Y*our perception of reality is built upon all sorts of automatic thoughts such as these. It is built upon seeing how other people respond to you when you do certain things. It pays attention to the ways in which you interact with the world in certain situations. It acknowledges that you are navigating the world through the experience that you have built up over time, allowing you to recognize what it means to behave in certain ways.

*E*verything that you ever experience goes into shaping those perceptions of reality that you have. From how you grew up to the problems you have faced throughout your lifetime, all of those go right into you understanding the way in which you interact with the world. They all shape that perception; they all mold that idea that you have in the world. If you have experienced that spiders are scary, every time that you see one, you will navigate as if that spider is terrifying. It could be that you were bitten. It could be that you saw someone else panicking over a spider. It could be something that you learned about spiders that made them scary in the first place. That perception of reality that you have built up is what leads to that fear of the spiders of the world.

*Y*ou will develop perceptions about just about anything that you encounter; while people do not like to admit it, we are quite likely to make our own judgments about the world that we experience. We are constantly judging everything as these evaluations are created and then applied, and very quickly, we suddenly have our own mental images of the world around us and how everything works based upon those judgments that you have made. This is crucial for you to remember; you must be able to acknowledge these points. When you can acknowledge what is going on, you can begin to see the ways in which you interact with the world. You can begin to understand this to allow you to better see the ways that you navigate the world. These judgments and the perceptions of reality become the way that you do manage to interact. They guide you. They all come together to create your mental maps.

*T*he Mind and Mental Mapping

When you gather up all of your perceptions about reality, you come up with what is known as mental maps. You are constantly mental mapping—this involves you creating the way in which you can navigate the world around you. It creates the ways in which you are able to better understand the world around you and how you navigate everything that you do explore within your world.

· · ·

*W*hen it comes right down to it, you create these maps that dictate the way in which you interact with the world based on those perceptions. These maps will show you what it is that you must do to better work with the world around you. When you work through the world based on the mental maps that you create, you can know that you are essentially following your programming.

*R*emember that the mental maps that you create are the internal processes that you have that influence your behavior. These maps are going to dictate the way that you interact. This means that your gut reactions are always influenced by the ways in which you can see the world around you. They are determined by the perceptions that you build over time. When it comes down to it, then, these are what really make up who you are and what your tendencies become when you do navigate the world around you. You must be able to ensure that your own mental maps, then, are healthy if you want to ensure that you have healthy behaviors.

*U*ltimately, the mental maps that you have are also found within your unconscious mind. They exist underneath your perceptions, just far away that you are able to understand and make use of them. When it comes down to it, you must be able to really stop and reflect on the world around you to then develop that understanding of yourself and how you will need to change your own thoughts if you want to change the directions that exists within that mental map that you have.

NLP and Using Mental Maps

The mental maps that you develop are, thankfully, something that can be influenced relatively simply. Whether you choose to influence your own mental maps or to influence the mental maps of other people, the same fundamental concept applies: You are constantly living somewhere within your own mental map. Your perceptions of reality will constantly shape the world that you live within and to expect or assert anything different would be remiss. This means that you have to accept that the world that you live in, or rather, the perception of the world that you live in, is inherently different than that of your neighbor's. Your own life experiences and your upbringing will change everything and you will never have the exact same perception on something that someone else would have. This is a major problem when it comes down to understanding other people; you must be able to recognize that no two people will have that same mindset and that means that no two people will ever be regarded as truly able to agree.

This can have other problems as well; if one person's mental map is so incredibly skewed from past traumas or problems, what can be done about it? How can you begin to repair those skewed beliefs or images that are developed in hopes of ensuring that the individual is not so negatively influenced? How can you ensure that you, or someone else, is able to find that healthy mind map build?

Ultimately, you can learn how to influence these mental maps. You can learn how you develop that change in the ways that you interact with the world and you can learn to alter those mental maps, either through coaching or through making use of other methods entirely. This means that you can better begin to regulate the ways in which you interact. There are several

key ways in which you can begin to influence the mental maps of
either yourself or others.

*F*irstly, you can pay close attention to broaden those
mental maps. If the mental maps are built up in a very
narrow context, you can work to begin to broaden them out to find
more effective ways to help those that must learn. You can essentially begin to stretch out that mental map that has been developed. If it is your own map that must be expanded upon, you must
look at the ways in which you see the world around you. Look at
the interactions that you have. Look very closely at the way in
which you see the world around you, and you are likely to figure
out the problems that you will have. In doing this and slowly
expanding your mental maps to become something that exist
within a less narrow constraint, you can usually allow yourself to
stop and see that, at the end of the day, you dilute the negative or
problematic maps and perceptions that you have.

*S*econdly, you can try to work within a mind map instead.
You will take the time to consider what is happening
within the mental map rather than attempting to expand it. When
you address the situation directly from within the mental map, you
can then begin to determine how to change it. You can start to
influence that mental map, especially if you are able to get control
of what is going on around you. When you develop that influence
over yourself or over the mind of the other person, you can begin
to redirect that mental map. As you better influence the metal
map, you can develop the necessary understanding that will be
required for any sort of successful mindset that you could have.

. . .

$\mathcal{F}$inally, you can also influence the mind through the use of other NLP techniques that are not necessarily inherently designed to influence the mental map, but that will absolutely do so. In making use of NLP for yourself, you can develop a sort of flexibility for your own mindset; you can develop the power that will enable you to better control the way that you are thinking and ensure that you can better adapt to other, more beneficial mental maps instead.

$\mathcal{W}$hen it comes right down to it, you can test if your mental map that you are making use of is actually constructive through self-reflection, or through reflecting on other people and their own mental maps. When it comes down to it, the easiest reflection that can be done is whether or not one's world view is one that will bring joy or pleasure to one's life. Is it going to allow for happiness? Is it satisfying? Are you genuinely enjoying the life that you have or are you constantly feeling like you are trapped or stuck in conflict?

$\mathcal{W}$ith an inefficient mental map, you will struggle, or the other person will struggle. It is impossible to get through life happily and healthily with a normal, well-adjusted attitude. This is not because of you or your own shortcomings, but rather because you are going to have a skewed worldview. You need to learn how you can realign that worldview if you hope to be able to truly be comfortable in your own skin or the world that you live within.

THE UNCONSCIOUS MIND

UNDERLYING everything that makes you who you are is the unconscious mind. The unconscious mind is there to ensure that, at the end of the day, you must pay closer attention to the ways in which you are interacting with the world. You must be able to control the ways that you behave somehow, and the way that is done is through the use of how you are able to control yourself. When it comes right down to it, you need a way of processing everything that happens within your mind and that is primarily done through your unconscious mind.

The unconscious mind must be able to work with itself; it is able to keep you breathing as you sleep. It is able to keep you responding to the world around you. It prevents you from acting in ways that are going to be detrimental for you. It creates your emotions to help to convey ideas to your mind. It does all of this and more, constantly working as a sort of unseen guide behind the scenes.

· · ·

*T*he unconscious mind is like your puppet master—it pulls all of the strings that make you act. It controls everything that you do without thinking about it. It creates those impulses that you feel. It creates those innate desires that become too difficult to resist, such as feeling as if you must be able to better interact with those around you. It controls the way in which you are able to do just about anything at all and in doing so, it becomes the most important component when it comes to the behaviors that you have and what you do with your own life.

*W*hen it comes right down to it, when you are navigating through life, your unconscious mind is what is going to be your guide. It will keep you from getting into danger. It will detect problems that you have and attempt to influence the way that you behave to ensure that you are kept safe. It will help you to prevent yourself from regretting your behaviors. It exists as something that you are never really aware of, and yet, it is more powerful than the other areas within your mind. It is easy to think that you are only ever learning consciously; after all, you are used to the idea of only being a conscious being. You are used to only being able to access the parts of your mind that you are aware of, and yet, there is so much more underneath the surface.

*J*ust like with icebergs, there is so much more beneath the conscious mind. There is so much more going on in terms of what makes you what you are and who you are than just your conscious thoughts, and when you can acknowledge that, you realize that you must be more mindful of those unconscious thoughts. It is only when you discover what is really going on underneath the surface. Upwards of 90% of your mind exists in levels that are not being used, underneath the conscious mind that you are aware of.

The Conscious vs the Unconscious Mind

The conscious mind is easily defined through the use of awareness. When you are aware of what you are doing, you are taking a look at the complex behaviors and processes that the brain is capable of within its conscious processes. The conscious mind, while the only one that you are really cognizant of in the moment, is not actually the majority of the processing that your mind does. Most of the processing is done in other aspects of the mind instead. The conscious is responsible for your conscious thought, logical thinking, critical thinking, long-term memory, and that willpower that you must exert when you feel the urge to do something that you know would not actually be beneficial to you at the end of the day. When it comes right down to it, it becomes important for you to recognize that you do, in fact, keep up with what you are doing.

Underneath that consciousness, however, there is so much more going on. You must be able to take a look at everything else that must happen in order for your mind to process anything. These are your automatic thoughts that occur, your habits and emotions, and more. These are meant to be automatic and require less processing power; this is because conscious thought requires so much attention and so much awareness that it is incredibly demanding. If you had to consciously process each and everything that you do throughout your day, you would be horribly inefficient. Just think about it—what do you have to do in order to do that is habitual and automatic? What it is does not matter—just think about something simple. Perhaps it is the simple act of brushing your teeth. Think about what you have to do to brush them—you have to put the toothpaste on the brush and then you brush, right?

*T*here are actually many, many other actions that go right into it as well. You must be able to recognize that you are also working hard to scrub. You must remember the way in which you move your hand forward and back, but also remember that you would have to consciously grip what you are holding onto as well. Keep in mind that you would have to also be able to change the way in which you move your arm, tensing different muscles. It would be horribly inefficient to have to consciously activate each and every one of these muscle groups and because of that, you also have your unconscious mind there to make the situation simpler for you. It controls those habits to protect you.

*M*any other processes occur similarly. Your values, for example, are driven by deeply held beliefs that you may develop over time. These beliefs are designed to allow yourself to better understand what matters to you. You have them to help make snap judgments about the world around you. Without those automatic thoughts about your beliefs, you run into other problems as well; you can run into issues in which you are unable to really process what is going on. For example, imagine that you have a belief that all good dogs that you pass walking down the street deserve a good pat on the head and a treat. When you walk down the street, then, every time that you see a dog, you feel compelled to treat them in this manner. You can see this with other processes as well; imagine that you are of the firm belief that people around you deserve to be treated with respect. Without thinking about it, you will naturally do so.

This is the power of the unconscious mind. It makes habits out of those beliefs that matter to you the most. It makes sure that, at the end of the day, you are satisfied with what you are doing. It makes sure that you can cut down on the conscious thought that you need to follow through with. You must be able to recognize that at the end of the day, your unconscious thoughts matter and if you cannot admit that, then you will run into other issues. The unconscious thoughts are those that make up your mental maps and you must be able to see that.

*I*ncluded within the unconscious mind are actions such as your beliefs and emotions, your habitual behaviors, the values you live by, and intuition. You also must recognize that this part of your mind is also responsible for ensuring that you are kept alive. It includes your visceral, protective responses to the world around you. Imagine, for example, the ways in which you respond when you feel threatened. Imagine the ways in which you feel when you are told that you are failing or that you are betrayed. Think of those visceral gut reactions that come along when you need to protect yourself. Those, too, are the creations of your unconscious mind.

PROGRAMMING YOURSELF

PROGRAMMING YOURSELF DOES NOT NEED to be difficult. It does not need to be something that you are worried about doing; at the end of the day, with a few simple considerations, you, too, can take complete control of yourself and ensure that you are better able than ever to lead the life that you want. Within this chapter, we are going to look at how you can take control of that power for yourself. You are looking at the methods that you can use to ensure that you do, in fact, get the power that you are looking to obtain. All you have to do is make sure that, all things considered, you are better able to recognize the patters that you need to follow.

*W*ithin this chapter, we are going to address the ways in which you can work to program yourself. Oftentimes, NLP is learned and developed with the sole intention being to take control. It is designed to allow for the development of the beliefs and habits that you need. You are in charge of yourself. You can learn to control your mind—the conscious and the uncon-scious. You can learn how you can take control of the patterns that you live by, rewriting that map once and for all and ensuring that you do, in fact, develop the understanding that you need to change who you are, how you behave, and more. It is simple to learn and, so long as you are willing to do so and put in the effort, NLP can become an incredibly useful tool to aid you in your own personal self-development.

What NLP Targets

When it comes to programming yourself, there are three ways that you will really be able to aid yourself in becoming the best version of yourself that you can become. You can develop the state that you are looking to master. You can work on your story that you tell of yourself. You can change the strategy through which you work through life. In targeting these, you can make the changes that you want to have.

Changing your state

NLP firstly works to change your state- this is your emotions or mood that you are in at any point in time. When you have that in consideration, you need to realize that, ulti-mately, the way that you interact with the world is determined entirely by the way in which you engage with the world. You can recognize that your state, that emotional feeling that you have at any point in time, is directly related to the ways in which you interact with the world and then, that consideration means that you will also be able to figure out how best to change them. You know that your state will influence the behaviors that you have, sometimes in very dangerous ways, and that can be a huge problem for you. You must be able to take control of everything that you have going on. You must be willing and able to take complete and utter control over the mindset that you have. In learning NLP, you will get that power.

Changing your story

*N*LP will also aid you in changing your story—this is the narrative of the life that you have lived so far. Usually, this narrative is highly corroded or highly corrupt. It could be that you are not thinking about the way in which you are behaving. It could be that you think that the way that you have lived your life is actually more of a problem than it actually is. It could be that your story has become some sort of excuse for why you cannot take control in the first place. However, you can reframe that story. You can rewrite the way that you talk to yourself and if you do that, you know that you can better work on the ways in which you talk to yourself. You can develop the ability to better work with other people. You can show yourself the ways in which you are able to control yourself. You can ensure that, ultimately, you do remember that you must keep track of the way in which you talk to yourself and if you can reframe everything, you know that you are able to better work with yourself so your future behaviors can fit what you wish to do in life.

*C*hanging your strategy

· · ·

*F*inally, you can use NLP to help you change your strategy. The strategy is the mental map that you develop; it is that way of thinking that you will need to follow if you hope to really be able to take complete and utter control over the thought processes that you have to follow. When it comes down to it, the strategy that you follow, those mental maps that you create, will control everything. No matter what it is that you want in your life and no matter how much you wish to change what is happening, you want to ensure that you can, in fact, change them. It will not be easy—but it is something that you can do. All you have to do is work to defeat the habits that you are likely to have developed during the course of time that you have done so. If you can work to change your strategy, you can then begin to work to change your behaviors.

*T*he Keys to Developing Yourself

What you must do if you wish to develop yourself is to work hard to implement the principles of NLP. You must work hard to ensure that, ultimately, the way that you attempt to approach the world around you is appropriate for what it is that you hope to achieve. Ultimately, what you want to achieve is dependent upon yourself and what it is that you seek to achieve. To develop yourself, you must be able to implement certain patterns and steps to ensure that you can change yourself and your thinking. You can become more positive and effective in your life; you just have to try.

. . .

To do this, you must follow a few keys and make them your way of life.

Understand your patterns

This is learning to recognize what you are doing in the moment. If you want to develop yourself, you must learn to read yourself and how you behave. Usually, we all have habits that can become problematic for us. You must be able to recognize what those problematic habits are and how you can better understand what is going on within you. You need to understand the fact that your thoughts will create feelings and your feelings will create the behaviors. When you see the ways in which your entire being is driven by those thoughts, feelings, and behaviors, the habits that are led become far easier to identify. You become capable of seeing the ways in which you behave and the ways in which you must change yourself to fix the problems. When you can begin to understand the way that you behave and understand how they originate, you are well on your way to developing yourself with NLP.

Change your patterns

You must, after identifying your patterns, learn to change them. You can either enhance the ones that are working for you, allowing yourself to better yourself and ensure that you choose behaviors that work for you, or you can try to change the patterns that you live by. When you are able to get in and either confirm or deny those patterns, you begin to see the changes that you are looking for, whether those changes were continuing to follow those behaviors or changing those behaviors to become something that is easier than ever to follow along with, you will know that you are better prepared. You will know that you are more likely to succeed. The changes of the patterns are the catalyst to get that lifestyle that you are looking for.

Communicate better

In the process of changing yourself and your patterns, you begin to communicate better as a direct result. That communication that you live by becomes easier than ever and if you can develop those better behaviors, you will know that ultimately, you are more prepared than you thought to ensure that you do live those positive behaviors. When it comes down to it, you must be able to communicate, both with yourself and with others if you hope to keep the process working for you.

Achieve your goals

The next key point that you must ensure to follow is to achieve your goals. Remember, NLP is highly driven by goals. If you are not careful and you do not try to do so, you are likely to struggle to meet those goals and that is a problem. However, remember that you can develop the ability to achieve them if you take the time to do so. You can change your behaviors to ensure that, ultimately, you *can* become the person that you want to be. You can motivate yourself to succeed if you take the time to do so and that is highly powerful. In working to achieve your goals and ensuring that you continue to think about that achievement, no matter how you approach your life, you will be able to better thrive.

Recognize your mind's language

*Y*ou must also be able to stop and understand the language of your mind. Remember, language is a major component of this all and if you do not keep that in mind, you will not succeed at what you need to do. You will not be able to keep yourself successful if you are not paying attention to what you need to do and how you tell yourself about it. You must always spend the time to understand the way in which your own mind operates so you can understand what to expect with yourself. You must be willing and able to recognize the ways in which you speak to yourself if you hope to be successful and that involves the use of learning to master the use of language and change it to something that is more beneficial to you.

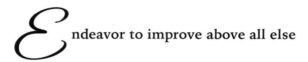

*E*ndeavor to improve above all else

· · ·

inally, when it comes right down to it, you must also be able to improve yourself. You must approach everything as if you are attempting to improve. You must have the mindset that you can improve if you hope to do so. If you cannot keep yourself in that mindset that you can do better and that you will do better, you likely will fail to do so at all. You must be able to recognize that, ultimately, the way that you control yourself and the way that you think about yourself matters greatly.

PROGRAMMING OTHERS

PROGRAMMING OTHER PEOPLE IS, in some aspects, simpler than trying to change your own programming just because it is easier to subliminally influence the mind of someone else without them really being aware of it than it is for you to wholeheartedly convince yourself of something that you do not actually believe. This is incredibly important to remember and you must keep in mind that ultimately, when you wish to change the mindset of someone else, that you have a clearly defined thought process for doing so. You must know what you are doing, how you are doing it, and why it matters to you. If you can do that, then you can change anything about the other person that you really wanted to.

*W*ithin this chapter, we are going to take a look at the methods with which you can program other people. We are going to look at the three primary criteria to remember when you are trying to change the mindset of other people. Like with programming yourself, there are certain aspects that you must keep in consideration. You must remember that you can change their thoughts, their stories, or their strategies, much like how you can change your own. The only trick here, however, is that you must also remember what it will take for you to better program them.

*R*apport

Rapport becomes the most important factor of all when it comes right down to being able to program other people. You cannot program them if you cannot develop that necessary rapport with them. If that rapport is not developed, then any attempts that you make to attempt to alter the mind of those around you will fail. This is simply because of the fact that you are likely to run into all sorts of alternative problems You are likely to find that, no matter what happens in your relationships with that other person, if that rapport is lacking, so too will that influence.

*W*e will be addressing the development of rapport within the next chapter, allowing for a more thorough understanding of how to do so in order to ensure that, ultimately, you will be able to better control everything that you are facing. At the end of the day, you must be able to recognize that your ability to develop that rapport is crucial. You must be able to ensure that you can better deal with the other person through the development of that connection with them. When that connection is built up, you will better be able to ensure that ultimately, you are successful. All you have to do is work hard. If you can do that, you can know that ultimately, your success matters greatly. You will be able to ensure that ultimately, you will better deal with the problems that you face with other people.

．　．　．

*R*eally, rapport works, then, as a way to sort of disarm the unconscious mind. It allows for you to slip past the conscious mind's firewall, so to speak; it will allow you to discover what truly matters and how you can really become capable of controlling yourself and controlling those perceptions that people have of you. When you develop that control and that sort of hidden entryway into the other person's mind, you can know that ultimately, you will be successful. All you have to do is find that sort of back door in the first place. When you can identify it, you will have the access and the rapport that you will need for the other steps.

*U*nderstand the Other Person

Next, you must work to understand the other person. What is it that makes them work? What makes them tick? How can you better understand what is going on in their minds? Can you allow that understanding to aid you in other attempts to understand them? Can you allow that understanding to help you to become better equipped with understanding the problems that you will face at any point in time? When you can understand the mental maps of other people, you begin to recognize their values. You learn to read their minds; you learn to see what matters to them and what does not.

*T*his is perhaps one of the more critical skills that you will need here; without this skill, you cannot discover what it is that you need to change in the first place. This is essentially learning to read people and learning to recognize their own actions and how they relate to the individual that you are attempting to understand. Typically, this involves trying to track backwards across the individual's own actions and tendencies. You will essentially be trying to discover what it will take for you to ensure that you are able to manage your own understanding of the person so you can use that to manage their behaviors as well.

*E*ssentially, you are looking at the thoughts, feelings, behavior cycle to create inferences about the other person, their mindset, and what you can really expect from them at the end of the day. You must be willing and able to see the ways in which you can better process everything that is going on with them. You start this out by looking at body language. Body language itself is a nonverbal form of communication. You must recognize the body language of the other person so you can then begin to understand what is going on in their minds as well. The sooner you learn that, the sooner you can make great progress toward controlling them and their mindsets.

*T*he body language will usually be your way to explore the unconscious mind of the other person. The unconscious is highly responsible for this body language; it is unconscious communication that your mind is giving out in an attempt to control what you are doing and how you are doing it in the first place. When you are able to focus on this, you can better ensure that you make the right decisions at the end of the day because you do get that insight.

*T*he body language will always betray emotions thanks to that connection to the unconscious mind and that means that what you are looking to do is develop and understanding between the unconscious mind of the other person and what they are doing. You must stop and consider what they are attempting to convey. You must be able to ensure that you do develop that time and energy toward doing what you need to do to understand them. What does their body language tell you about their current feelings? Is it open or closed? Is their body language something that you can trust your reading of, or is it something that is going to need to be reevaluated? When you have a good reading of their body language, you can then move over to understanding their emotional state as well.

*W*hen you understand their emotions that they are feeling, you can start to piece together everything that is going on around them. You can observe what is going on and what seems to have triggered those feelings. You can figure out what it will take to really understand what is going on in their minds from the other end as well; this will allow you to better process everything that is happening entirely. You will be able to understand the ways in which you are able to better recognize their feelings that they have and in recognizing their feelings, you can begin to recognize the thoughts that underlie those as well.

*R*emember that our thoughts are our sort of mental framework and when you can start to understand those in other people, bit by bit, you can usually better understand what is going on. You can begin to recognize it all; you can see why and how people respond the way that they do. You may catch onto patterns that they themselves are woefully unprepared to face, or you may find that ultimately, you are simply following your own intuition on the matter to try to better understand what is going on or why it is happening in the way that it is. You must be willing and able to consider this and consider what it is that you will do with that knowledge.

*U*ltimately, NLP is learning the innate undertakings of someone else's mind. It is learning to see the world through that other person's eyes with your own perspective. It is learning to understand what is going on with the other people in their side of things, learning to see what really matters the most and how that can be utilized better than ever to ensure that at the end of the day, people will be able to understand what is going on. It is crucial to being able to understand what is going on and how you can alter the thought processes of other people. When you have that, you know that you can succeed in altering their mindsets.

*O*f course, this takes practice. It takes a lot of foresight, hindsight, and even empathy to develop this understanding of other people. It is not always easy to recognize what is going on in their minds, nor is it always something that you really want to be able to do. At the end of the day, you must be able to really understand what is going on and how it is happening. You must be able to see the world through the eyes of the other person and recognize the ways in which you can interact with those around you. When you develop this, and when you develop your ability to better understand these other people, only then can you begin to truly make use of NLP to rewrite their minds.

Guide the Other Person's Mind

When it comes right down to it, once you have that understanding of the other person, you can then begin to guide the minds of the other person. You can then begin to recognize that ultimately, the way that you process the understanding in the other person's mind is entirely the way in which you interact with them. You are able to recognize that, at the end of the day, you do realize that you are interacting with people in very intimate manners. You are learning to guide their mindsets and with that comes a requirement for you to also respect the understanding that their minds are their own.

*N*evertheless, sometimes, people benefit from having their minds guided. Sometimes, they need to have that experience pushed in order to ensure that they are better able to control the way that they think. When you learn to do that and when you learn to ensure that you do properly keep this in mind, you know that you are making the right decision. You know that you are more likely to be choosing to influence the minds of other people in a way that is beneficial to them.

*W*hen it comes down to it, you must ensure that you influence people based on what is going to be best for them. This is primarily through the use of identifying somewhere within their own current mindsets that you can see there is a big need for change. You must be able to implement that change carefully, ensuring that ultimately, you do figure out what you need to do to fix the problem at hand. When you learn to do that, you can learn to recognize and influence the way in which you interact with them.

*Y*ou begin by identifying the goal that you wish to lead with. What is it that you want to change for the other person? You must have something going on within that understanding of them and their mindsets that will be important for you to understand. Then, you must ensure that you are able to recognize that ultimately, you do need to understand them and their mindset to succeed. When you can implement that goal and make the changes with the techniques that you will be discovering shortly, you will begin to see the changes that you were looking for.

RAPPORT

Rapport becomes one of the most important aspects of any relationship with someone else. Whether you intend to make use of NLP or not, rapport is like that measurement of what is going on within someone else. It is that understanding of everything that makes them who they are. It is seeing the ways in which you can better understand how to implement the changes that you are looking to see in people around you. When you develop a rapport with someone else, you get that necessary bond that will guide the way in which you interact with them. You will develop that ability to ensure that you are able to really control the interactions that you lead with those people that you are around.

Rapport is about more than just tricking someone into allowing you to really understand them. It is more than ensuring that ultimately, they will follow your lead. It is about learning what it is that is going through the mind of the other person. It is developing that relationship with them that will bind you together. It is about learning what really makes people tick underneath everything else and understanding it is one of the greatest things that any aspiring NLP practitioner can learn. If you want to learn NLP for other people, you must be able to interact with people with ease. You must be able to work well when it comes right down to it. You must ensure that ultimately, you are working hard to ensure that you can better control the way in which you interact with others.

What is Rapport?

Rapport is that connection that you build up with someone else; it is that state in which you and the other person have an intimate understanding of one another. It is the feeling of just clicking with the person that you are talking to, or being able to trust what those around you are saying. It is that feeling in which you are able to really recognize how much you like someone that you are interacting with. It is a measurement of the trust that you develop for those around you and that is something that is highly important, especially in NLP.

When it comes right down to it, however, rapport is little more than a bond between two people. It is that sense of connection between yourself and the other person; it is your ability to feel bonded to that other person and to feel like ultimately, you have no choice but to react with them. You share their feelings through empathy. You see their joy and feel it, too. You understand their thought processes. When you are able to develop that rapport, you know that you are developing a connection with someone. You know that you are able to ensure that the relationships that you have are genuine and in doing so, you know that you can trust the other person.

. . .

*T*ypically, this is done through all sorts of methods. Early on, it may be in realizing that you and the other person share a close sense of humor. It may be that you and the other person are highly compatible in other ways, such as sharing the same worldviews. You could even have experienced something together that was enough to create that beginning of the bond in which you and the other person were able to better connect with each other. When it comes right down to it, the rapport that you build with someone else is special. It is powerful. It is necessary, and without it, you will struggle with NLP.

*R*apport and NLP

Rapport matters in NLP because it allows you and the other person to develop trust. It tells you that the other person is paying attention to you; it reminds you that the other person does see you as trustworthy and in trusting you, you are able to help persuade them and guide them through their own behaviors. It gives you that power that you need. It gives you the ability to ensure that at the end of the day, you can master the art of influencing other people.

*N*LP requires rapport because it is unconscious. It is something that the other person does not think about. They simply trust you and they follow your lead on an unconscious level. Look at how two old friends walk together; they follow that same pacing with each other. They stay on the same path with each other. They ensure that they are able to properly follow each other around. They do all of this through the use of making sure that they are able to really recognize the way that they interact. They are able to guide themselves and see that at the end of the day, they should be trusting you. When you can establish rapport with someone else, you are able to bypass their conscious detection; essentially, you are deemed to be trustworthy. The other person is not on guard around you and that means that you are able to begin influencing them.

This is often done through modeling—which oftentimes involves making sure that the other person moves with you to repeat the same behaviors that you are attempting to encourage. Essentially, you guide the other person into following your lead because you want them to follow along. You want them to change their behaviors to those that you can trust to be similar to you and in doing so, you know that the other person is more likely to follow along at the end of the day.

Developing Your Own Rapport

Rapport is developed either naturally, through time that you spend with someone else that you like, or it can be facilitated through other methods as well. If you pay attention to the way in which you interact with people around you, you will be pleased to note that you are not going to have to work hard to develop rapport the natural way. You will simply want to spend some time really interacting with other people. You will want to take your time to really interact with people in meaningful manners. You want to make them like you and because you want to make them like you, you try to be like them in the first place. After all, it is far easier to be able to like someone that is similar to you, right?

However, sometimes, you do not have the benefit of time to help you really work better than ever. You need to ensure that you are able to make those proper bonds with other people. When you want to develop those bonds with other people, you simply need to know what you are doing. They are not too hard to force into existence if you are able to ensure that you know what you are doing. No one can fault you for needing someone else to get into your skillset at some point in time or another. When you need that rapport, however, there has to be a solution that will work for you, and you must be able to find what it is to ensure that you can get that rapport rolling when it is needed the most.

*T*he quickest way to develop rapport is through mirroring. Mirroring will allow you to really push that rapport to build up the way that you have been needing to see it. When you can develop that rapport through mirroring, you can usually do it during the course of a conversation, especially if you and the other person already seem to be on the same page to begin with.

*W*hen it comes down to it, building your rapport is crucial and it all begins with mirroring. Remember, mirroring is all about empathy. Mirroring is triggering those same mirror neurons to ensure that they are working for you so at the end of the day, you will be able to properly mirror someone else to get them willing and able to mirror you as well. You can make this happen somewhat simply as well if you are able to pay closer attention.

· · ·

*T*o begin, you must firstly engage with the person that you are hoping to mirror. Who are they? What are they doing? What matters the most when it comes to that interaction with them? How can you really facilitate that interaction with them in the first place? Recognize who they are and sit down for a conversation. Ideally, they should be the one doing all of the talking. If you can ensure that they are the ones talking, you can usually just nod your head along with them while really working hard to facilitate that bond yourself. To do so, you must go through a few simple steps.

*A*s your conversation continues, make sure that your body language says that you are listening. Face the other person. Ensure that you are square to them and nod your head as you listen to them speaking. These nods should come in series of threes—this usually can hint to the mind of the other person that you are listening, paying attention, and recognizing that you are in agreement with them. This is important to establish—remember, people like those that they agree with because there is a common ground that is present.

*Y*ou should then focus on convincing yourself that you like them. Make sure that if you are trying to convince them, you are spending the time necessary to ensure that you are able to better process your need to relate to each other. When you can ensure that you relate to the other person or that the other person is likable for you, you can usually convince yourself that the rapport is there, and that rapport gets mirrored back to you.

As you listen to the other person talk as well, you will naturally engage with them. You will naturally be involved in the conversation that you are having with them and that leads to you being able to better understand and relate to the other person. How can you ensure that, at the end of the day, you are in agreement? The best way to do so is through essentially mirroring the talk. You want to mimic their speech to allow you to facilitate that connection; you are ensuring that they see that you are in agreement with them because you are mimicking their speech patterns. Some people recommend that you mirror body language, but that is usually too on the nose, and when people notice that you are intentionally trying to make them like you or intentionally trying to convince them to listen to you, you are not usually going to have a very good time. This can be a huge problem for many people; it is essential that you avoid being seen as trying to force the point or you may be deemed a manipulator or someone else that is equally as dangerous. You must attempt to make your attempts to interact with the other person as smooth and painless as possible if you want to ensure that, at the end of the day, you are able to process that rapport, and that means that you must ensure that it remains undetected.

When you want to mimic the vocal patterns that someone else is exhibiting, there are a few key points to consider; you must consider firstly their tone that they are taking. Are they serious or happy? Are they casual or formal? Copy their general tone and vocabulary preferences as you talk to them for the best luck here. Then, you must also consider the speed at which they are talking as well; you should attempt to match their pace. You must also work to ensure that you are able to talk to them at paces that you know that they will be very receptive to in order to ensure that you are able to better understand the way in which you interact with them. You must ensure that your attempts to interact with those around you are successful and the only way to do this is by matching their vocal pitches at this point in time.

*W*ith the voice mimicked for a while, it is time to identify what is known as the punctuator; this is the particular motion or phrase or intonation that you notice that someone uses like an exclamation mark. You want to essentially find their way of showing extreme emphasis on something when they are talking to someone else and when you can find that, you can usually also ensure that you will better connect to that other person. You will ensure that you are better able to relate to them and this is best done by mimicking that punctuator. When you mimic it, they will catch on to the fact that you are relating to them. They will see that, ultimately, you do share that connection and that you can make great use of it.

*W*ait for the next chance that you get in your conversation where you believe that they are about to use the punctuator. Then, you want to activate it yourself as well. When you do that, you ensure that you are able to better connect and better relate. At this point, their unconscious mind gets it; they see that connection between you and the other person and they are going to make use of that. You then want to ensure that you interact better with them. All you have to do is make sure that you are willing and able to follow along.

. . .

*W*ith that done, you test it. All you have to do to test it is ensure that you make some small movement and see if they do the same thing. You may, for example, brush a hand through your hair or shift your pose. Do this and see if they do the same. If they do, you will know that they are mirroring you. This means that you were successful. If they do not mirror you, however, you have failed and you will need to try again.

*Y*ou may need to try a few times before you establish that rapport with someone else, but generally speaking, if it is not present after several attempts, it is not likely to develop at all and that will mean that you need to give up on the idea. You may need to, for example, attempt to talk to them some other way or let the rapport develop naturally. It may just not develop at all. Try and set your mind to it. Also remember, if you do not feel the connection, they are not going to feel it either. This is just as much about getting that connection for yourself as it is getting them to feel it as well.

UNDERSTANDING VISUAL, AUDITORY, AND KINESTHETIC CUES

BEFORE YOU BEGIN MAKING use of the NLP techniques that you are going to be learning shortly, you must firstly take a look at the representational systems of NLP. These are the learning styles that each person has and each person is going to learn slightly differently from everyone else. No matter if you are teaching children, adults, or anyone else, you are going to want to keep these styles in mind. Generally speaking, the three most prevalent learning modules are visual, auditory, and kinesthetic. You want to follow these along as much as you can and if you can figure out the VAK (Visual, Auditory, Kinesthetic) style that they use, you are going to have a better chance of getting through to them.

*J*ust as people tend to learn differently and some people may find that they have great luck with talking to someone else while others prefer to get information written down for them instead, and others still prefer to do something to understand it, people can be influenced by NLP differently depending upon their styles as well. You will want to identify the ways in which you can better understand these people so you can then begin to better recognize their actions and how to influence them. If you can get that down for yourself, you will be able to better interact. You will be able to better guide them. You will be able to identify how to reach out better than ever before, and this book is going to teach you how to do so now.

Visual Learners

Visual learners are people that are typically able to understand and learn very well by seeing things done for them. They find that they are able to learn the best when they watch someone else do it first. When they are able to watch someone else's behaviors, they learn what it is that they should be doing better than if someone attempted to talk them through it. For these people, you want to model what it is that you want them to do. You want to ensure that you are developing that rapport and then acting it out for them. If you want them to stop biting their nails, for example, every time you see them getting close to biting, you would pace and lead them away from such a behavior. You may also use the use of your own body language to change their own body language and therefore their emotions as well.

There are several telltale signs that the individual that you are interacting with are visual learners, including:

- They speak rapidly and jump around a lot as they speak—they are usually thinking visually and that involves a lot of jumping around from scene to scene, not unlike a mental movie on their end

- They tend to think about the big picture to help them make decisions
- They typically prefer to meet and interact in person as opposed to over email or from person to person
- They typically wind up speaking at a higher pitch, and when they are breathing, you see the movements in their chest as opposed to the belly.
- They sit upright and their eyes usually point upwards as they visualize
- They rely on gestures widely
- They are quite organized, neat, and typically present themselves cleanly and well-groomed
- They struggle with being told what to do; they need things written out for them
- They usually use expressions related to sight (I see, I get the picture, etc.)

When you are interacting with someone that is visual, you, too, will want to tap into those sight-related cues; talk to them using expressions that involve and imply vision, such as "I see what you are talking about." This helps them to activate their own learning and activates their attention. You will also want to incorporate body language regularly.

Auditory Learners

Auditory learners, on the other hand, need to hear what they are doing. They explore the world based on what they hear, how people talk to them, and how they can hear themselves. They are entirely focused on remaining engaged in conversations, for example, and they may express a preference for audiobooks or watching and listening to the news rather than reading a newspaper. People that are auditory learners typically:

- Are rhythmic in their behaviors and movements
- Speak at average tones in their voices
- Are aware of the changes in their voices as well as in the tones of those that they are talking to
- Are distracted in loud environments
- Usually are skilled at repeating back what has been said to them
- They converse regularly and listen well
- They usually tilt their head to the side as they listen
- They usually memorize things in the order that they were provided
- They like to hear feedback
- They breathe in the middle of their chests
- They use expressions that imply listening, such as, "That clicks for me," or "I hear your side of things."

These people require you to engage with them in vocal manners. They are going to be best lead by you speaking to them and using techniques such as weasel words or other auditory methods of trying to influence them. You can change their perceptions by the way that you present your speech to them.

Kinesthetic Learners

Finally, kinesthetic learners are those that learn by doing. They need to actively do something before it really clicks for them; they will often follow along with a tutorial while acting out the motions themselves. They may use their hands to move from direction to direction when they are being told how to get somewhere or where something is. They rely heavily on the movements of their body to help them recognize what is going on around them.

. . .

*U*sually, these people are easily recognized by the way in which they engage with those around them. They will often make use of their bodies far more often than other people and they will do things such as:

- Speak slowly because they need time to connect those words to what they are doing.
- Speak with a lower, deeper tone that is more filled with vibration, and they usually pause regularly in their conversations
- They learn through actively doing something as opposed to through other methods
- They typically will require physical contact as feedback
- They usually ensure that they are comfortable above all else
- They usually decide based on intuition and gut feelings
- They position themselves closer to those that they are interacting with
- They learn through actively following along to ensure that they know what they are doing and how to do it
- They usually speak with metaphors implying touch, such as getting a hold of someone or getting in touch with them.

These people usually allow themselves to figure out the world around them through the use of their sensory data and they require that sort of physical connection to other people or they will struggle. You will be best served relying on other methods to really relate to those around you, including methods that will imply that you are closer to them.

. . .

*W*hen it comes right down to it, the ways that you tend to interact with those that you are attempting to influence and control will be directly related to their sensory preferences. By emphasizing them and ensuring that you do choose to follow those regularly, you know that you will easier to understand to that person. They will better learn from you if you are able to activate their learning styles and that can be a huge difference between whether your attempts to influence them are successful or not. If they are, then great! If not, you need to figure out what else is going on and how you can better make the entire situation work better for you. Sometimes, it just takes a shift in perspective and learning techniques to really get through to the other person, especially if you are aware of your own preference and therefore can tell when you are slipping into your own defaults instead of relying on what they have to say about it.

NLP TECHNIQUES FOR YOURSELF

NOW, we are going to take some time to go over a few of the most useful techniques that you can use in NLP to help you reframe yourself. These methods will usually allow you to better process what you are doing in order to try to change your mind and therefore your experiences. You will find that these methods can greatly change the way in which you interact with the world around you and they can greatly aid you when it comes down to bettering yourself. We will go over four key methods that you can use for yourself here.

Dissociation

Have you ever felt like you wished that you could just disappear? It is commonly felt when you are in pain—either physically or emotionally. No matter the kind of pain, you know that you would be best served being able to escape the pain, but despite your best attempts to do so, you find that you cannot? This happens to all of us sometimes, but NLP can allow you to do

exactly that. NLP can teach you how you can progressively disso-
ciate yourself; this is a great tool if you, for example, have a
migraine. If it is your emotions that are the problem, you can
follow the same principle, but make sure that you frame the way
that you speak to yourself to accommodate accordingly.

*Y*ou are going to slowly but surely step further and
further away from whatever your problem is so you
can better cope with it in the moment. Let's imagine,
for the moment, that you are suffering from hurt foot. Perhaps you
sprained your ankle on your morning jog and it really hurts. You
are now trying to make the distance between your mind and that
pain as far away as you can possibly manage to help yourself better
cope with it.

*T*his is a very simple process; you start by identifying the
pain. Where is the problem? It could be in your heart. It
could be your head or your foot. Identify the source of the pain and
then target it for a moment. Ask yourself how it feels? How is your
foot feeling right that moment? How does your foot feel about the
pain?

*Y*our foot probably hurts a lot, but beyond hurting, you
tell yourself that it does not think anything at all; it is
a foot, after all. Now, shift your attention just a little
bit further away from your foot. Now ask yourself how your calf is
feeling about it. What does your calf currently feel? Does it like the
pain? How is it dealing with it all? You will probably once again
tell yourself that your calf does not feel anything and that it is not

capable of thinking at all, meaning that it entirely lacks a perspective on what is going on.

*Y*ou will continue to move further and further away from the point that is hurting you. How does your thigh feel about your ankle's pain? What about your hip? Your stomach? Your back? Your shoulders? Every step that you take away from the pain in your foot should help to distance yourself and dull the pain that you are suffering from. M0ve beyond yourself as well —how does the world feel about your pain that you are feeling? What does that pain do t you from the perspective of others? How does that pain influence the ways in which you behave? How does it influence the ways in which you are likely to be interacting with the world around you? How is it that you can learn to recognize what really matters for yourself and how you can take care of it?

*B*y the time that you start asking about how the world around you feels about your pain, you often find that you are so distanced from the paint that was plaguing you that it is no longer a problem at all. You either have dulled the pain somehow or you have removed it entirely, learning how you can remove yourself from dwelling it and therefore changing your thought process. You are changing the narrative behind the pain of your ankle; you are reminding yourself that the pain is not a big deal and that you will be fine distancing yourself from it.

ontent Reframing

Content reframing is another exercise that you can use

that will allow you to essentially reprogram the way that you are thinking. It is teaching you to stop and look at your thoughts from a different position entirely. It helps you to discover that you can change your perspective and when you change that perspective, you change everything else, as well. You are able to change the content that you have in your mind through the use of looking at the world around you. You are able to change the way that you think about what has happened, rewriting the story and the narrative behind what you normally feel and how you normally behave.

*W*e all have these narratives within us; it simply becomes a matter of being able to change that narrative entirely. When you are able to defeat that narrative you can then begin to make the real, true progress and change that you have been dying to see in life. You can then begin to recognize the ways in which you are better able to see the world. This is a visualization technique that you can use to allow yourself to remove the victim narrative that you may have been living by for far too long. It is a great one for those who have suffered from stress, abuse, or illness and it is a great way to begin to dull the pain of trauma.

*C*ontent reframing typically happens in one of two ways— you either change the content or you change the context. One of the two gets reframed into something that will work better for you at the end of the day. The end result is that you are able to change the way in which you interact with the world around you and in doing so, you defeat the problems entirely. You can do this through the use of all sorts of visualization practices. When you change the content, you want to change the meaning of the situation that you were in. You are attempting to alter the focus within the memory to instead involve a different focus. This is usually through the use of shifting your attention to something that is not the primary focus most of the time. Shifting the context, then, is your other option. When you make use of this process, you are usually looking at attempting to focus on something entirely different within what you are looking at. You may be looking at the perception and shifting it into something positive. Instead of seeing the entire thing as a problem, you begin to recognize that there was a lesson to learn, for example.

*T*o do this, you must firstly identify whether you are reframing the content or reframing the context. Then, you must begin to figure out what is going on within that traumatic memory that you have? You would need to think back at the situation, thinking heavily about the memory. Maybe you slipped in mud in the middle of a rainstorm and you were really embarrassed because, for the rest of the year, you were known as muddy butt by all of your classmates in elementary school. It was horribly embarrassing and the nickname made it worse, especially as it continued to follow you. From that day on, you have found that your anxiety in the rain is far more than usual, and that you are generally nervous about interacting with people because you do not want to make yourself vulnerable to that kind of bullying or badgering again in the future.

*T*o reframe this, you must stop and think about the memory. Think about what it was that happened in your memory. Imagine the scene in your head as clearly as you can—you can see yourself falling, landing in the mud, and you can feel just how wet your pants were as you sat in the giant puddle of mud. You know how the children around you made fun of you. However, to fix the problem, you must look for something else that you can pay attention to. Reconsider the situation entirely—things could have been worse, right? What if someone else had fallen in the mud? What if someone else had gotten hurt instead? What if you had fallen and landed on someone else instead and hurt them? You stop and consider the many different ways that the problem could have played out and you focus on something positive—your mother picked you up from school and took you out for hot chocolate after you got all cleaned up, and that allowed you to get more time in which your mother than before. That could be a great way to think about this memory, for example.

*B*y shifting your focus of that memory from what had happened and associating that rainfall with the problem that you faced into instead focusing on something good that came out of it, you can begin that reframing process. Perhaps, you start to focus on rain being connected to that nice mug of hot chocolate that you shared in the café with your mother. Maybe you remember the fun that you and your mother had together when you did go together. This allows you to stop and realize that things were not as bad as they seemed. Things could have really been a whole lot worse, but they were not.

*T*his allows you to begin pushing past the idea of you being a victim. It starts to focus on something that matters to you; onto something that is positive and enjoyable and that is a great thing to remember. When you shift your attention like this, you know that you are better able to process the situation around you. You now that you are better able to allow yourself to interact with that memory and you learn how to distance yourself from that negativity entirely.

· · ·

Anchoring

Anchoring yourself is perhaps one of the most versatile methods that you can use when it comes down to NLP. When you use anchoring, you are essentially conditioning yourself to feel or think a certain way when you do something in particular. For most people, they choose to anchor a very specific action to a very specific behavior or feeling that they need, such as for anxiety or for other stressors that you may face.

At the end of the day, when it comes right down to being able to manage your stress, the best way to do so is through learning to tame it. Imagine that you are always quite stressed out and when you are stressed over what you have to do or how much you have going on, you start to panic. That panic obviously does nothing to really help you learn how you can fix the problem, but you cannot defeat it. However, you can learn how you can make a different connection to what is going on. You can learn to defeat that anxiety through the use of the anchors that you develop. All you have to do is choose the anchors that you want to use for yourself.

If this sounds vaguely reminiscent to a high school psychology class, that's because it is—you are making use of classical conditioning here. Imagine that you want to defeat your anxiety. To do so, you want to remind yourself of feelings of calmness whenever that stress happens. When you feel your stressors starting to escalate, you need to identify a way that you can fix the problem and you choose to do so through the use of relaxation.

· · ·

*W*ith that in mind, you must also choose an anchor for yourself. Perhaps you chose to make it fiddling with a necklace that you have. Perhaps you choose to pay attention to the way in which you move your hand or an attempt to tap on your arm. No matter the method, all you have to do is be consistent with it. With your method for anchoring and your target feeling identified, you are ready to begin.

*S*top and think about a time in which you very strongly felt the emotion that you are trying to connect to. It could be your own happiness or anything else. In this instance, you are looking at connecting to your feelings of calmness. You think to a situation that makes you feel calm it could be your wedding day or it could be a night that you spent out, underneath the stars, with your best friend. No matter what it is, however, you know one thing: You are feeling calmer already. Really focus on that memory that you have until you, too, being to feel just as calm as you did that night. Focus entirely on how calm you felt and then, as that feeling maxes out, you must use the anchor. It could be touching your necklace or it could be tapping your hand or making a certain gesture. Do that now, as you feel calm.

*Y*ou will need to repeat this process several times over the coming days. Make sure that, every time that you begin to feel really calm, you use that motion or gesture and you latch onto that feeling of calmness. Then, allow yourself to really feel it as you anchor it.

. . .

*O*ver time, you will find that you do feel calmer than ever. You will find that you do feel better and that you are certain that, at the end of the day, you have done what you needed to. You will then want to try using your anchor to see if it works for you. If using your anchor then immediately triggers those good feelings for you, you know that you have succeeded. If it does not, however, you know that you will simply keep working and keep being consistent with it.

*Y*ou can also anchor actions to your gestures as well you can train yourself to do just about anything if you pay attention to what you are doing and try hard enough. This is strongly recommended; you should absolutely try to make use of this if you can and if you do it correctly, you will be able to defeat any negative feelings that you may have otherwise had.

*B*elief Changes

Finally, belief changes are the last of the methods that we will consider within this chapter. To change your beliefs, you will want to begin to acknowledge them. Remember, your beliefs that you have are generalizations. They may be entirely flawed, especially if they are negative beliefs that are not helping you at all. If you are suffering from negative beliefs, it could be well worth the time and effort of doing so. You are able to stop, recognize the negative belief, and then recognize how that negative belief is actually a problem. Then, you must be able to make sure that you make the changes.

· · ·

*T*his particular shift in thinking is all about changing your thoughts. It is as simple as correcting yourself when you do notice that you are engaging in negative thoughts that are not helping you at all. If you negative thoughts are doing nothing but hurting the way that you are able to interact with the world, then you know that you have no choice but to change them. Changing them is all about correction.

*E*very single time that you catch yourself thinking those negative thoughts, correct them. Do not allow them to linger and do not allow yourself to entertain them. Simply erase the thoughts from your mind and ensure that, at the end of the day, you will be able to fix the problem. It all begins with the change of one belief. When you reprogram that one thought first, challenging it regularly, you will then realize that something wonderful will happen as a result—you will realize that, at the end of the day, you can fix the problem entirely. You can ensure that you are able to control the way of thinking that you had and in doing so, you can then enable you to better deal with everything.

NLP TECHNIQUES FOR OTHERS

WHILE THIS BOOK is not entirely meant to indulge in the idea of NLP as a form of mind control, it can be used to directly influence the way that those around you are thinking. It is quite simple in the way that it does so, as well. It is usually able to engage in the way that other people are thinking, changing the mind and subtly and subliminally interacting with them. When you do this, you are able to slowly but surely influence how those around you are reacting.

*a*s has been mentioned already, if you want to be able to engage in the use of NLP on other people, you must remember that you need to pay attention to the rapport that you build with other people. It is really only when you are able to really understand the other person and really recognize that the other person also trusts you that you can begin to make good, solid use of the NLP techniques that you would otherwise be reliant on. At the end of the day, you must be confident in the ways in which you interact with those around you to ensure that you are better able to understand how to influence them.

*W*e are going to take a bit of time to consider three ways that you can begin to influence the mind of others with ease. These are not difficult methods—but you will need to consider the fact that they must also ensure that they are able to change the way that you think. You must remember that they are persuasive in nature; you are not controlling someone's mind so much as influencing them to see the world the way that you want them to.

*S*peaking at the Heart's Rate

The heart's rate of somewhere between the speed of 45 and 72 beats per minute is perhaps the most persuasive, suggestive speed that you can choose to deliver the use of the speech that you attempt to influence other people with. You can make use of this speed to ensure that you can suggest to other people what they should be thinking or feeling. This is literally just as simple as slowing down to this rate, perhaps with gentle eye contact and also ensuring that you pay close attention to the ways in which you interact with those around you. It is crucial that you are able to recognize the skill that this speed can be used with and how you can really begin to get people to follow along with you.

*U*sing Hot Words

The use of hot words is just a bit different than many of the other uses of language that you have seen so far. This works to develop rapport rapidly and effectively by virtue of the ways that you choose to talk to those around you. Typically, the hot words that you will use are those that are directly related to the senses. Remember, we experience the world through our senses. It is through the senses that we feel that we are able to really explore the world around us and how we are able to interact with it, and because of that, this becomes one of the most influencing ways that you can talk to someone else.

*U*sually, this is used through the use of the hot words that will align with the other person's closest learning preference. If you are talking to someone who learns best through auditory methods, for example, you would be heavy handed with the auditory expressions and words that you used. You would make use of words such as, "hear me out," or "hear my side of things," or "are you hearing me?" Someone who is more likely to be a physical, kinesthetic learner, on the other hand would be better influenced through the use of words that would appeal to the use of language that involves the physical senses. You may say, "Feel free to notice..." or "Are you feeling it?" By shifting to these touch-based methods instead, you are able to really influence the way that the other person chooses to relate to you. This allows you to better understand the way that you are able to recognize the way in which you interact with the other person.

*K*eeping in mind that everyone has their own sensory preferences, then, you are able to remind yourself precisely how those around you should be spoken to if you take the time to remember how to tell the sensory preferences apart. Take the time to stop and consider the ways in which you can learn to recognize these preferences. Commit them to memory because being able to understand the thoughts behind someone else's mind is a crucial skill that everyone needs to develop. If you can do so, you know that you will have a better chance at being able to deal with the problems at hand. You will also be able to convince people of doing whatever it is that you really want them to do, all by ensuring that you tap into their sensory preferences in just the right ways to ensure that you do know how to influence those around you. This is highly powerful.

Using Your Body

The body is highly convincing and when it comes right down to it, when you mirror someone else and then lead them into an action, you can change the way that they think with ease. All you have to do is ensure that when you do lead them, you are making it a point to lead them well. One of the most common methods of doing so involves the use of nodding to directly influence the way in which they think or feel. You may want to ask someone a question, for example, that you want them to say yes to. The best way to influence them into saying yes, then, is to nod your own head—subtly of course—as you ask the question. It should not be particularly noticeable to the other person and it should not be something that they are likely to recognize without seeing the way in which you are interacting with them. However, when you do ensure that you do this, you will usually get them to nod along with you. Remember, the unconscious mind is always watching, and when you do this, their unconscious mind is going to pick up on it. Their unconscious mind wants to nod along with you because it also wants to mirror you back. This leads to you being that much more likely to get them to say use to you, all because you nodded your head subtly as you asked them your question that mattered to you.

. . .

*P*ace and Lead

Another way that you can use your body is known as the pace and lead method. This method involves you stopping to spend the time to pace and lead the other party. You are essentially matching the other person's body language before then making use of it yourself. You are attempting to control the way in which you interact with the other person, matching them first, and then taking the lead.

*I*magine, for example, you want to lead the walk that you are taking. You want to go at your pace, wherever you want to go. The most natural way to take control of this is to match the pace of the other person as well as you can, ensuring that you are walking with them. Walk at the same pace, breathe with them, and move your arms at the same pace. This is a power-play move that will ensure that, ultimately, you are able to better pace to the other person.

*A*s you match their pace, their mind catches the mirroring that you are doing. You can then ensure that you take control. You can start to slow the pace down. You can slowly change the way that you are walking and watch as they match pace to you, continuing to keep that status quo of mirroring you so you can take control. You then shift over into other methods as well; you make it a point to, for example, ensure that you are better able to control the other person. You make it a point to, for example, watch as you change the way that you behave in hopes of taking control of them and the walk itself. If you did your job right, you will notice that you are in complete control of the walk.

. . .

*Y*ou can use this premise in other ways as well. You can, for example, ensure that you are better able to allow yourself that control over those around you. You can, for example, pace someone into saying yes to something. You can use the pace and lead to get someone to change their body language as well, such as in negotiations, to then create a more open mindset for them. The options that you have are nearly limitless.

*U*sing Leading Words

One last method that we will consider, then, is the use of leading words and leading phrases. These are quite similar to the way in which you would use hot words, but unlike hot words, you are relying on the fact that the other person is going to hear your suggestion and naturally answer the question that you have asked as opposed to the one that you are implying.

*C*onsider this situation for a moment—you really want to go on a trip with your spouse. Instead of asking if you two can go, you can ask your spouse instead, "When should I buy the tickets for this event?" You never asked if your spouse wanted to go with you; rather, you bypassed that question entirely in preference for identifying the question that you really cared about. Your question that you asked implied consent already and your spouse will likely not pick up on this. Rather than being direct with asking permission, you skip the problem entirely and that means that you are much more likely to get what it was that you were looking for.

CONCLUSION

Congratulations! You have made it to the end of *NLP*. Hopefully, as you read through this book, you learned all about how you can make use of these techniques for yourself and how you will be able to ensure that you can change, not just your own mindsets, but the mindsets of those around you as well. You can learn to tap into the power of NLP to ensure that you are the one in control of yourself. You can learn to ensure that, no matter what happens and come what may, you will be able to restructure your own thinking.

The skills taught within this book and understanding how you are able to control yourself and your own feelings are crucial for anyone. No matter who you are, being able to control your emotions is something powerful that you should not be willing to give up too easily. You must ensure that you can develop that ability with ease, and the best way to do so is through the use of NLP practices and ensuring that, no matter what happens, you are able to recognize that your changes that you will make will make a real, big difference in life. You must ensure that, no matter what happens, you remember just how useful NLP can be. You must be able to recognize the power that it can hold, not just over yourself, but also over those around you.

From here, all that you have left to do is ensure that you are making the changes that you want to see in your life. From here, it is time to ensure that you are taking action. You are beginning to identify the problems that you may face in your life. You must be able to understand how NLP works and how that can guide you in understanding what matters. You must be able to recognize the power that your unconscious mind has and how you can make use of it, as well as how you can begin to not only influence yourself, but those around you as well. You can use these methods to change your own thought processes with ease, or you can choose to apply them to other people instead. You can learn how to build a rapport with someone else and then begin to change the pacing of a conversation or get someone to give you want you wanted, or you can use these methods for anchoring yourself to feeling more confident in your life. No matter how you use it, NLP can be influential and life-changing for anyone.

Thank you for taking the time to read through this book, and good luck on your future endeavors as you head out into the real world with this book as your guide. Please keep in mind that these techniques are highly powerful and you will be able to take control of yourself with them and do not forget just how potently powerful they will be when it comes down to changing the way in which those around you think. Finally, if you found this book useful in any way, a review on Amazon is always appreciated!